WILL TO WIN

BY MIKE KLIS OF THE DENVER POST

ABOUT THE AUTHOR

Mike Klis covers the Denver Broncos for The Denver Post. The oldest son of Joseph and Mary (Ann), Klis is a graduate of Oswego (Ill.) High School and Murray (Ky.) State University. He got his start as a sports writer with the Oswego Ledger-Sentinel, where he covered high school sports and the town's men's slow-pitch softball league. He later worked in Colorado for the Fountain Valley Advertiser, Woodland Park's Ute Pass Courier and Colorado Springs Gazette Telegraph. He joined The Denver Post to cover the Colorado Rockies baseball team in January, 1998. Klis moved from the Rockies beat to the Broncos beat in July 2005. Klis and his wife, Becky, have four children: Brittney, Kaitlyn, Blake and Johnny.

ACKNOWLEGDEMENTS

This book would not have been possible without the contributions of these fine journalists at The Denver Post: Scott Monserud, Assistant Managing Editor/sports; John Mossman, sports copy editor; J. Damon Cain, Managing Editor for Presentation & Design; sports columnists Woody Paige, Mark Kiszla and Dave Krieger; Broncos beat reporters Lindsay H. Jones and Jeff Legwold; photo editors Dean Krakel and Meghan Lyden; Tim Rasmussen, assistant managing editor for photography; photographers Joe Amon, Hyoung Chang, Andy Cross, John Leyba, Steve Nehf, AAron Ontiveroz, Helen H. Richardson and Craig F. Walker; photo technicians Glen Barber and Werner Slocum; and Linda Shapley, director of newsroom operations.

E-BOOK

Purchase an electronic copy of this book, suitable for viewing on different tablet platforms, at www.bookbrewer.com/denverpost.

Created and distributed through bookbrewer.com

COPYRIGHT 2012 THE DENVER POST — ALL RIGHTS RESERVED

No part of this book may be reproduced or transmitted in any form or by any means, electronic or mechanical, including photocopying, recording, or by an information storage and retrieval system — except by a reviewer who may quote brief passages in a review — without permission in writing from The Denver Post.

The Denver Post, 101 W. Colfax Ave., Suite 600, Denver, Colorado, 80202 303-954-1800

Front and back jacket photos: John Leyba, The Denver Post

CONTENTS

CHAPTER 1, PAGE 4
TEBOW "PULLS THE TRIGGER" AGAINST STEELERS, REIGNITING MANIA

CHAPTER 2, PAGE 14
COMING SOON: THE GUY WHO COULDN'T THROW STRAIGHT

CHAPTER 3, PAGE 28
HE WAS THE COMEBACK KID, DETERMINED TO PLAY QUARTERBACK

CHAPTER 4, PAGE 40
A GREAT COMPETITOR, A WINNER, A LEADER. BUT CAN HE PLAY IN THE PROS?

CHAPTER 5, PAGE 50
IT WAS ELWAY WHO SUGGESTED THE CLOCK IS TICKING TOWARD TEBOW TIME

CHAPTER 6, PAGE 60
YES, TEBOW WAS UNCONVENTIONAL. BUT, HE BEGINS WINNING OVER TEAM

CHAPTER 7, PAGE 74
FAITH IS TEBOW'S ROCK. BUT SOME CAN'T RESIST CASTING STONES

CHAPTER 8, PAGE 84
STATS WERE ADDING UP AGAINST THE IDEA OF TEBOW AS SAVIOR; OAKLAND ON DECK

CHAPTER 9, PAGE 98
RESPECT HIM OR NOT, CHANCES ARE PRETTY GOOD THAT YOU HAVE HEARD OF HIM

CHAPTER 10, PAGE 108
WHILE ELWAY CATCHES WRATH OF FANS, TEBOW, BRONCOS GO ON A WINNING STREAK

CHAPTER 11, PAGE 118
MOMENTUM SWINGS AGAINST THE BRONCOS AS DEFENSES FIGURE OUT TEBOW

CHAPTER 12, PAGE 128
TEBOW WILL NEVER PLAY QUARTERBACK, RIGHT? THAT'S WHAT THEY KEEP SAYING

CHAPTER 13, PAGE 136
PROGRESS, A PLAYOFF WIN AND GUTTY DETERMINATION EARN TEBOW THE 2012 NOD

WILL TO WIN: CHAPTER 1

TEBOW "PULLS THE TRIGGER" AGAINST STEELERS, REIGNITING MANIA

Following 60 minutes and 11 seconds of game-time decisions, Tim Tebow was finally drawing a blank. The Broncos' quarterback had just zipped a pass across the middle to his favorite receiver, Demaryius Thomas.

It was the first play of overtime, and from what Tebow could tell, Thomas was running with the ball. Where, exactly, Tebow didn't know. The crowd roar sounded promising, but from where Tebow stood, he couldn't see his talented buddy.

So, Tebow did what he often does when he doesn't know what else to do: He started running.

"I couldn't see with the angle I had, so I was running and then he's in the end zone, and you go, 'What?' " Tebow said. "Thank you, Lord! That was the first thing I thought."

Tebow was delirious with joy. He kept running toward the south end zone of Sports Authority Field at Mile High, thanking the Lord every couple of strides or so. The sellout crowd of more than 75,000 stood – cheering, jumping, hugging each other. Familiarity with the person nearby was not a prerequisite.

The pass play from Tebow to Thomas officially traveled 80 yards and gave the Broncos a stunning, 29-23 overtime victory against heavily favored Pittsburgh in a first-round AFC playoff game Jan. 8, 2012.

Make that play about 120 yards. After Thomas crossed the goal line, he kept running. A la Bo Jackson, Thomas ran through the end zone, through the opening

TIM TEBOW SPRINTS DOWNFIELD, CELEBRATING THE GAME-WINNING TOUCHDOWN AGAINST PITTSBURGH. *AAron Ontiveroz, The Denver Post*

leading up to the tunnel, and on up through the vacuum to what was now the victorious home locker room.

And now, for one final time, Tebow would make a decision on the fly.

"I had no idea what I was going to do," he would say later. "I was just running. And then I couldn't find anybody once I got to the end zone. Everybody was in the tunnel or something. So I just jumped into the stands. That was kind of cool. First time I had ever done that. And the fans were so excited. It felt good, but they were so excited, I didn't know if they were going to let me go."

Tebow laughed as he was talking, chuckling with that wonderful boyish, innocent laugh of his.

The CBS network cameras covering the game missed Tebow's Mile High Leap. They did catch up to him in time for the namesake to "Tebow" in the end zone.

He dropped his right knee to the ground, bent his left knee up, bowed his head on his right hand and said a quick prayer.

"Thank you, Lord!"

What did Tebow do right there? The nation knows it as "Tebowing."

The game ran long – even though overtime lasted just 11 exhilarating seconds – so CBS had to cut away quickly to feed the local news or "60 Minutes." Given just a few seconds to wrap up the game, "The NFL Today" studio crew of James Brown, Bill Cowher, Dan Marino, Shannon Sharpe and Boomer Esiason dropped into a "Tebowing" pose on the set as they signed off.

To some, it was a cute way of honoring the hero of the day, the story of the NFL season. To others, the analysts made a mockery of Tebow's unblushing Christian belief.

And so it goes with Timothy Richard Tebow.

• • •

He has become one of the most adored, and criticized, athletes on the planet. He is a proven champion with a perpetually uncertain NFL future. He is the quarterback who often puts a wobble in his throws, and a man with a heart so large it can beat into the other 45 Broncos on a game-day roster.

Earlier in the Broncos' wild 2011 season of winning streaks and losing streaks, devastating injuries and miraculous comebacks, trades and non-trades of star players, fans didn't just chant for Broncos coach John Fox to "Put in Tebow." They hung the message on a city billboard.

Tebow became not just a pronoun but a verb. If a team got beat late, it got "Tebow-ed." If a quarterback came through with a clutch, final-minute victory, he pulled a "Tebow." Starting with the week of Halloween, buddies in bars, kids in the school hallways, Olympic gold medal skiers on the slopes and people who just plain felt like it while walking down the street were "Tebowing."

For all his fame and victories, though, Tebow constantly had to deal with the harshest of insults: He'll never make it as a quarterback.

He couldn't play quarterback in Pop Warner. His first Pop Warner coach ignored Tebow's position request and played the big, strong kid at running back.

He couldn't play quarterback in high school. His first high school coach played him at linebacker, where the older Tebow brothers played, leading Tim to transfer to another high school.

He couldn't play quarterback in college. Tebow was panned as an ill-fitting SEC quarterback by sportswriters following his first Orange and Blue scrimmage at the University of Florida.

He couldn't play quarterback in the NFL. Before he entered the NFL draft, a highly respected former NFL coach-turned-analyst, Jimmy Johnson, suggested Tebow could make it as an H-back, but not as a quarterback.

And there was no way Tebow would be the Broncos' starting quarterback in 2012, no matter what he had done in 2011. Other Broncos quarterbacks got to start the season 0-0. Tebow took over a team among the league's worst at 1-4. Not only 1-4, but an NFL-worst 7-24 going back to Nov. 1, 2009.

And yet, Tebow stepped up to lead this group of undrafted rookies, unwanted free agents, aging veterans and unproven youngsters and guided the Broncos to their first playoff appearance in six years.

Along the way, he led the league in two categories: fourth-quarter

> "Honestly, I just don't worry about what everybody else says. You never know what your future holds. So I'm not going to worry about it.
> **I'm just going to play ball.**"
>
> **Tim Tebow,** on how he responds to criticism of his quarterbacking skills

WHILE THE STADIUM WAS ROCKING AFTER THE WIN OVER PITTSBURGH, TEBOW SAID A PRAYER. *AAron Ontiveroz, The Denver Post*

comebacks and wobbly passes. His last two games of the regular season had no comebacks and more ducks than a city pond.

Confidence in Tebow had so quickly evaporated by regular-season's end that heading into the Broncos' first-round playoff game, the primary question concerning his future wasn't whether he would be the team's starting quarterback in 2012, but whether he would make it through the Steelers game without being replaced by backup Brady Quinn.

As the Denver Post's Mike Klis wrote in his NFL column on the morning of the Steelers-Broncos playoff game Jan. 8:

Sam Bradford has played 11 bad games in a row.

Look it up. Yet, nobody questions whether he's the St. Louis Rams' quarterback in 2012.

Josh Freeman just lost nine in a row where he either recorded clunker after clunker or put up some phony garbage-time stats late. No one asks if Tampa Bay needs to find another franchise-type quarterback.

Tim Tebow has won more games (7) this year than Bradford and Freeman combined (5). Yet now that he's had two bad games in a row, the overwhelming sentiment says the gig is up. It's over for Tebow.

Why is that?

"It's hard to say," Tebow said Friday at his locker. "It's OK, though. Honestly, I just don't worry about what everybody else says. You never know what your future holds. So I'm not going to worry about it. I'm just

| WILL TO WIN: CHAPTER 1

TEBOW HAD SUCH A MISERABLE END TO THE REGULAR SEASON THAT SOME THOUGHT BRADY QUINN MIGHT GET THE CALL AT HALFTIME OF THE PITTSBURGH GAME IF TEBOW CONTINUED TO PLAY POORLY. *John Leyba, The Denver Post*

going to play ball."

But then Tebow paused and, as he so often does during interviews, thought about it some more.

"It's hard," he said. "It's harder than just saying it. It's hard to ... to live it, you have to really believe it. You have to just go play."

The No. 1 question pointed at the Broncos the past two weeks: Who is going to be the quarterback in 2012?

No, that's not quite right. The No. 1 question is more accurately worded: Let's say Tebow stinks it up against the Steelers. Then what do the Broncos do about their quarterback situation in 2012?

The question is usually stated matter of factly. As if it's a legitimate query. Who else confronts these glum hypotheticals? Is it because Tebow is so unconventional?

"That might be some of it," he said. "I don't think I'm that unconventional, though."

With Ben Roethlisberger sharing the same field in Denver today, maybe Tebow is right. Tebow's style will seem less unique today.

Still, by Friday, the people's confidence in Tebow grew worse as there was speculation he might not make it past halftime today, never mind opening day of 2012.

Here's what they should know: Even if the Broncos wanted to pursue a quarterback upgrade for 2012, their draft position makes it unlikely. The Broncos are picking no higher than No. 21 in the 2012 draft. With Oklahoma's Landry Jones following USC's Matt Barkley in deciding to return to college, there won't be an available quarterback worthy of a draft pick at No. 21.

There are now only two legit first-round quarterbacks – Andrew Luck and Robert Griffin III. Indianapolis has to take Luck with the No. 1 overall pick. RG3 probably won't get past Cleveland at No. 4 – which is why Mike Shanahan's Washington Redskins will be looking to move up from No. 6.

All the other quarterbacks available in the upcoming draft would be considered reaches at No. 21.

• • •

The Broncos' No. 21 position in the 2012 draft dropped to No. 25 after the win over the Steelers. The point was, Tebow was virtually assured of becoming the Broncos' starter in 2012. He would cement his position with his superb performance – through the air, no less – against the Steelers.

To begin what turned out to be the biggest week of his professional football life, Tim Tebow was unusually bummed. He had just come off back-to-back rough performances against the lowly Buffalo Bills and Kansas City Chiefs to close out the regular season.

Worse, the Broncos not only lost the regular-season finale to his recent teammate – and nemesis – Kyle Orton and the Chiefs, they lost by an embarrassing 7-3 score.

Tebow was a miserable 6-of-22 passing for 60 yards, with one interception and a career-worst 20.6 passer rating. To put 20.6 into perspective, a quarterback can go 0-for-10 passing, or even 0-for-20, and so long as there are no interceptions, the rating would be 39.6.

Rarely has a team which had clinched the division title been so somber the day after. On the Monday afternoon after the loss to the Chiefs, Tebow sat in the office of quarterbacks coach Adam Gase, watching his former Florida Gators play Ohio State in a bowl game. Normally an enthusiastic supporter of his alma mater, Tebow watched dispassionately as the Gators beat Ohio State.

Wrote Klis in his game story of the Steelers-Broncos playoff game for

TEBOW HAD TO KEEP HIS COOL IN THE POCKET AGAINST THE TOP-RATED DEFENSE IN THE LEAGUE. *Hyoung Chang, The Denver Post*

WILL TO WIN: CHAPTER 1

The Denver Post:

All seemed doomed, playoffs or not. And the Broncos' mood reflected it last week.

"I think that's fair to say," Tebow said in a quiet hallway outside the home locker room. "We were down, but it was like a focus and very intense frustration that we wanted to get back on the field to show that wasn't us. I feel like our attitude and mind-set kind of grew all week."

Tebow spent the early part of the week covering his ears from a deluge of insults from local and national media outlets.

Worse, Baltimore linebacker Terrell Suggs joined current players Steve Smith, Jermichael Finley and Joe Flacco in bashing Tebow, breaking the unwritten code already long-broken by former players.

"I don't get it," said Champ Bailey, the Broncos' star cornerback. "You can say it looks different or whatever you want. But don't say he won't make it. You don't do that. This is like a big fraternity for me. Guys who do that, I lose respect for them."

Tebow awoke from his doldrums on Wednesday, when the Broncos began their formal preparations for the Steelers. During practice, a horn or whistle will blow marking the end of one period and the start of another. Tebow, the gung-ho Joe College guy that he is, sprinted from station to station.

Everybody else walks or trots from one station to another. Tebow – after four preseason games, 16 regular-season games and 23 weeks of practice – sprinted from here to there. Between every period. At every practice.

"I wanted to be focused and have that game face all week," Tebow said following his postgame press conference. "Not that I wasn't enjoying it, but I wanted to have that focus and concentration all week."

Helping Tebow this week was a push from front-office boss John Elway, who advised his young quarterback to "pull the trigger."

• • •

Elway and first-year coach John Fox would zap a forceful dynamic into the Tebow story throughout the year. The setup: Tebow was drafted in 2010 by then-coach Josh McDaniels and general manager Brian Xanders.

Elway, who led the Broncos to back-to-back Super Bowl championships and has since had his bust bronzed in the Pro Football Hall of Fame, was not working for the team at the time Tebow was drafted. Elway had not worked for the Broncos since he retired in 1998 as the franchise's all-time greatest player.

When Elway was hired by owner Pat Bowlen in January 2011 to start repairing the damage McDaniels had done, his first move was to hire Fox as head coach.

Neither Elway nor Fox were emotionally invested in Tebow. They inherited him. And as a quarterback, Tebow was more an acquired taste than love-at-first-sight.

At times during the season, Elway and Fox would unintentionally say something about Tebow that either wasn't very flattering or not very supportive of the popular young quarterback.

And the comments would blow up. A blog here followed by chatter there, and by the time the comment came back twisted to Broncos headquarters at Dove Valley, Elway and Fox supposedly didn't like Tebow.

It was Elway who told Fox after Week 3 that he had better start getting Tebow some reps. It was Fox who changed his offense so it better suited Tebow.

Yet, much as Elway and Fox were accustomed to public relations, they were both rookies when it came to Tebow. Rule No. 1 when talking about Tebow: Whatever is said, there's a good chance it will be a headline. There will be a strong reaction.

By regular season's end, though, few people blamed Elway and Fox for any reservations they may have had about Tebow.

Wrote Denver Post football reporter Jeff Legwold on what went wrong against the Chiefs, and what Tebow and the Broncos could expect in their upcoming playoff game against the Steelers:

John Elway did try to warn most anyone who didn't cover his or her ears in that la-la-la sort of way. In his young career as a football executive, Elway has consistently said the biggest games in the NFL are won by pocket-passing quarterbacks.

And a Hall of Fame QB who had a penchant for a little thing called a comeback win might know a thing or three about winning games that mean something. So, despite the Broncos' emotion-filled ride through October and November, opposing defenses have made a statement in the past month. They do not believe Tim Tebow can lead the Broncos to a win from the pocket. So they have trapped him there, significantly limiting his dual run-pass threat.

"We were able to contain him," is how Chiefs interim coach Romeo Crennel put it Sunday.

In the Broncos' three consecutive losses to end the regular season, Tebow completed 30-of-74 passes (40.5 percent) with four interceptions and three lost fumbles. He has lost a fumble in each of the past five games. Cover up the name next to those stats and opinions may change about what they mean.

It's certainly disconcerting for the Broncos, given that their three straight losses have come against defenses that finished the regular season ranked 31st (Patriots), 26th (Bills) and 11th (Chiefs).

THE PATRIOTS BROKE THE BRONCOS' WINNING STREAK AND SENT DENVER INTO A THREE-GAME SLUMP. *John Leyba, The Denver Post*

WILL TO WIN: CHAPTER 1

> "When you get into these playoff situations, he's a good enough athlete, you know what, to pull the trigger."
>
> **John Elway,** talking to Woody Paige about what Tebow needed to do

On Sunday, they'll face No. 1.

The Steelers concluded the regular season as NFL leaders in total defense, scoring defense and pass defense. That's quite a trifecta, and theirs will certainly be the best defense Tebow has faced in his time as an NFL quarterback. They held Tom Brady to 198 yards passing this season, Matt Schaub to 138 and Andy Dalton to 135.

The Steelers will do what they do to keep Tebow in the pocket, and Tebow will have to try to win his first playoff game from there. You can't say you weren't warned.

• • •

After Legwold analyzed what had gone wrong during Tebow's three-game losing streak, Denver Post columnist Woody Paige took the next step of trying to find a solution. For this, Elway was summoned again.

Not only did Elway have a good idea of what a playoff quarterback had to do – throw from the pocket – he also knew what Tebow had to do once in the pocket.

Wrote Paige:

John Elway has been there before – and is there again.

The Duke of Denver's advice to young Broncos quarterback Tim Tebow for his first NFL playoff game Sunday: "Pull the trigger."

A year ago tonight, Elway, always a gunslinger, officially became the Broncos' executive vice president of football operations. Twenty-eight seasons ago, in his second season with the Broncos, Elway started his first NFL playoff game against, as irony would have it, the Steelers.

Elway knows exactly what Tebow feels like.

With Tebow at quarterback, the Broncos won seven of eight. However, they've dropped the last three. Tebow seems to have lost his confidence and has been tentative, or fearful, throwing the football, I suggested to Elway.

"That's human nature, especially when you're young, to become more cautious," Elway said. "He had a tough week before (the Chiefs game) against Buffalo. The key thing for (Tebow) is to go out, put everything behind him, go through his progressions and pull the trigger.

"When you get into these playoff situations, he's a good enough athlete, you know what, to pull the trigger. He's obviously upset with last week. He's already got an edge to him, so he's ready to go. I like seeing the edge. Oh, yeah. I actually love it. I have full confidence he'll bounce back and have a good week."

• • •

Not surprisingly, "pull the trigger" became the catchphrase of the week. It was said repeatedly, particularly on Denver's three radio sports stations, in the days and minutes leading up to the Steelers game.

Klis' game story continued:

Tebow didn't just pull the trigger. He started launching. Early in the second quarter, he unleashed a beautiful 51-yard pass to Thomas. One play later, Tebow threw a perfect 30-yard touchdown pass to Eddie Royal.

The run-and-chuck offense was getting warmed up.

On his next possession, Tebow connected with Thomas again, this time for a 58-yard pass play to the Steelers' 12. Two plays later, Tebow ran a quarterback draw off a four-receiver spread formation for an 8-yard touchdown.

The Broncos were up 20-6 at halftime, but Pittsburgh quarterback Ben Roethlisberger, playing on a severely sprained ankle, brought the Steelers back to a 23-23 tie at the end of regulation.

"Yeah, I've watched him come through in Super Bowls," Tebow said of Roethlisberger. "He's such a clutch player. He was clutch today."

Just as it appeared all was lost, Tebow delivered.

• • •

The overtime coin toss ("Tails," said Steelers linebacker James Farrior) went the Broncos' way ("Heads!" said referee Bill Winter).

Continuing with the game story:

On the first play of overtime from the 20, Tebow winged a perfect pass to Thomas, who was crossing from left to right. Thomas stiff-armed away from one defender, and outran another who had the angle. And kept on running until he left the stadium.

In all, Tebow went John 3:16. That's what he thinks when he hears three-sixteen, anyway. Broncos fans of all beliefs will remember Tebow throwing for 316 yards and two touchdowns, and running for another score, to barely outduel the courageous and playoff-tested Roethlisberger.

"He can still throw the ball better,"

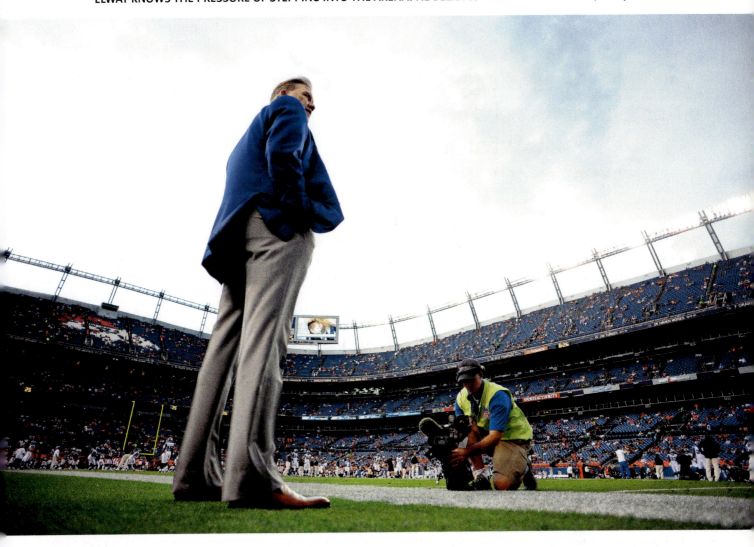

ELWAY KNOWS THE PRESSURE OF STEPPING INTO THE ARENA. HE BELIEVES HE CAN HELP TEBOW. *John Leyba, The Denver Post*

Broncos running back Willis McGahee said of Tebow. "It's not like he can't do it. He did it. But I know what they're going to say next week."

What's that?

"Can he do it again?" McGahee said.

• • •

The victory against the mighty Steelers validated everything about the Broncos' difficult, tumultuous season. It validated the hiring of Elway as the team's new front-office boss, even though the Hall of Fame quarterback had no NFL executive experience.

It validated the hiring of Fox as head coach, even though he had just gone 2-14 the previous year with Carolina. It validated keeping Xanders as general manager, even though he had worked closely with McDaniels.

Above all, it validated Tebow as an NFL quarterback.

"It's embarrassing to think the Broncos could win with Tebow!!" tweeted NFL analyst and former running back Merril Hoge on Aug. 3, 2011 – one week into training camp.

What's embarrassing is how much smarter Tebow fans are than so many pundits. When Tebow stepped into the huddle for the first play of overtime against the Steelers, over 50 million people were watching on TV. The average viewership that day, 42.4 million, made it the most-watched non-Super Bowl program since the Nancy Kerrigan-Tonya Harding figure skating event at the 1994 Winter Olympics. Kerrigan-Harding was a story of tragedy and so much of what was wrong with sports competition.

Tebow proved America can also be stirred by a story of inspiration. He represented so much of what this country wants from its sports heroes.

Against the predictions of nearly all NFL experts, Tebow and the Broncos were moving on to the second round of the AFC playoffs, and a rematch against Tom Brady and the New England Patriots.

WILL TO WIN: CHAPTER 2

COMING SOON: THE GUY WHO COULDN'T THROW STRAIGHT

On Jan. 5, 2011, three days after the Broncos finished their miserable 4-12 season with a home loss to San Diego, the greatest player in franchise history, Hall of Fame quarterback John Elway, was introduced as the team's new executive vice president of football operations.

The next day, his first full day as the Broncos' new boss, Elway was sitting behind his new desk facing Kyle Orton. The Broncos' incumbent quarterback asked for a trade. Orton wanted out.

Welcome, John Elway, to life as an NFL executive.

Orton did not want to deal with what star receiver Brandon Lloyd would later dub the "Tebow Thing." Tebowmania may be exciting in scope, but even 40 days of comfortably warm sunshine can leave a sunburn.

Orton felt like he was the guy getting burned by all the Tim Tebow excitement. He knew that even if he won the starting quarterback job for the 2011 season, the Broncos eventually would move toward giving Tebow a chance. Orton knew this because Broncos fans wouldn't let anyone forget it.

"He knew everything that was going on around us, so that's when he said he didn't want to be around it," Elway said from behind his desk near the end of the season.

From that moment on, the Broncos hoped to trade Orton.

"The plan going in was to see what Tim Tebow could do," Elway said. "The plan was to go into training camp with Tim Tebow competing with Brady Quinn

TIM TEBOW WAS ALL SMILES AFTER BEING DRAFTED WITH THE 25TH PICK IN THE FIRST ROUND BY THE BRONCOS. *Joe Amon, The Denver Post*

for the starting job."

There was only one problem with the plan: the NFL labor lockout. It began in March, when trades and a flurry of free-agent signings are normally executed. It lasted through April, when the league conducted its draft but didn't allow trades of current players. It carried on through May, erasing the team's offseason workouts, and through June, canceling minicamps.

Finally, on July 21, NFL owners ratified terms of a new 10-year collective bargaining agreement. Four days later, the players union agreed to the new CBA.

The Broncos, already behind other teams because their new head coach had never worked with them, asked their players to show up at the practice facility the next day, Tuesday, July 26.

Every player but Orton was there. Orton was told to stay home as the team tried to appease his trade demand. Initially, five teams communicated their interest. Orton, though, must have been everybody's backup plan because, one by one, teams in need of a proven starting quarterback quickly acquired somebody else. Matt Hasselbeck signed with Tennessee; Donovan McNabb was traded to Minnesota; Tarvaris Jackson signed with Seattle; and Arizona acquired Kevin Kolb.

The Dolphins, though, were interested in Orton enough to start the process of restructuring his contract, which had one year and $8.82 million remaining. While Broncos players "voluntarily" reported to the team's headquarters that Tuesday, Orton stayed behind as he and his agent, David Dunn, negotiated with the Dolphins.

By Tuesday night, Orton and the Dolphins were close to an agreement, according to sources, when the Dolphins began having second thoughts. A former fourth-round draft pick, Orton had been playing for "backup" quarterback money for five years, making $2.6 million in 2010. With $8.8 million coming his way in the final year of his contract and unrestricted free agency seven months away, he didn't want to surrender free-agent years for a pay cut.

The Dolphins couldn't acquire Orton for one year because they couldn't carry his salary against their cap. Orton decided that if he was going to play on a one-year contract, he might as well stay in Denver.

The deal appeared dead before it even reached the discussion regarding compensation. Contrary to several reports suggesting there was a hang-up about draft-pick compensation, the truth is the Broncos never made an offer. It never got that far. The Denver Post later confirmed that Orton and the Dolphins were working on the parameters of a three-year, $27 million extension.

Disappointed, the Broncos' brass informed Orton to report to work the next morning.

Tebow had no way of knowing, but in a matter of 24 hours and before he could throw his first pass of training camp, he had gone from being the starting quarterback to competing with veteran Brady Quinn for No. 2.

"My reaction? Well, time to go compete," Tebow said in a sitdown with The Denver Post after the season. "I wasn't down at all. You don't ever want to be handed anything. You want to earn it. Not, 'Hey, we're going to trade him and try to make it easier.' "

To be sure, camp did not open according to the Broncos' plan.

"I mean, two days before training camp, I'm assuming Tim's the guy," said Broncos coach John Fox. "You don't understand what we went through."

Even had Orton not asked for a trade, Broncos general manager Brian Xanders was in favor of moving him to clear the way for Tebow. Elway and his new coach, Fox, needed more time during the offseason to reach the same conclusion. They were new to their jobs and weren't as invested in Tebow, a prospect with unquestioned leadership and character attributes but a decidedly unpolished passer.

It's not that they doubted Tebow. They just hadn't been around him enough to form an opinion.

"You don't want to go in naive," Fox said. "You find out as much as you can. But at the same time, I've had people say they didn't like so-and-so, and then I met the guy and I liked him. And that's not football. That's anything. So you have to form your opinion."

Xanders was a different story. He joined the team as an assistant general manager in 2008 and became general manager in 2009. He was instrumental in the Broncos drafting Tebow with the No. 25 overall pick in the 2010 draft.

> "What Josh McDaniels saw in him God only knows. **Maybe God does know** – because the rest of us don't."
>
> NFL analyst and former quarterback **Boomer Esiason**, a Tebow critic

COACH JOSH MCDANIELS THOUGHT HE COULD FIX TEBOW'S MECHANICS. *Andy Cross, The Denver Post*

> "He had great college production. **His leadership and character were off the charts.** We were aware of the mechanical passing issues like everybody else. But Josh was confident he could coach him and fix him."
>
> Broncos general manager **Brian Xanders**

"He aced the interview and had a great workout," Xanders said. He and then-coach Josh McDaniels visited Tebow in Florida three days before the draft.

"He had great college production," Xanders said. "His leadership and character were off the charts. We were aware of the mechanical passing issues like everybody else. But Josh was confident he could coach him and fix him."

As the 2010 season went south, McDaniels made tentative plans to play Tebow in the final two games, both at home. The first would be against Houston, which had one of the NFL's worst defenses; the second against AFC West rival San Diego.

McDaniels, though, would not be around to implement his plan. Owner Pat Bowlen called McDaniels into his office at 4 p.m. Monday, Dec. 6. Bowlen thanked McDaniels for giving it his best shot, but the team was going in a different direction.

There were many reasons why McDaniels was fired before he could complete his second season,

The low point on the field was a 59-14 home loss to Oakland on Oct. 24, a game in which the Broncos fell behind 38-0 midway through the second quarter. A majority of the sellout crowd left at halftime. Nothing gets an owner's blood boiling quite like money flying out the door long before a game is finished.

The second satchel of misdeed heaped on McDaniels' ever-collapsing back was his admitted coverup of an illicit videotaping incident involving his close friend, Broncos video coordinator Steve Scarnecchia. Suspiciously, the incident occurred the week after the Raiders debacle. Scarnecchia taped six minutes of a San Francisco 49ers walkthrough practice on the eve of the Oct. 31 Broncos-49ers game in London.

When The Denver Post broke news of the illegal taping, the NFL acted swiftly, fining McDaniels and the franchise $50,000 apiece. (The Broncos fired Scarnecchia, concluding after an internal investigation that he acted alone; McDaniels admitted guilt to not reporting the incident.)

Although the videotaping scandal didn't directly cause McDaniels to lose his job, his days at Dove Valley were numbered. The Broncos had long prided themselves on building an organization of class and success, going back to their first Super Bowl season of 1977. They had had only five losing seasons since 1976 and appeared in six Super Bowls since then, winning two.

But under McDaniels, the team had lost 17 of 22 games after he started his tenure 6-0. McDaniels, the coach who most believed Tebow could succeed in the NFL, was gone. Running backs coach Eric Studesville was named interim head coach for the final four games of the 2010 season.

In Studesville's first game, the Broncos got hammered 43-13 at Arizona. Orton threw three interceptions and lost a fumble. Late in the game, he suffered what the team identified as a rib injury. The season was a disaster.

Studesville announced the day after the beatdown in the Arizona desert that Tebow would finish the season as the starter. Orton's injury was not a factor in the decision. Management wanted Tebow to get some playing experience. Fans made it clear they wanted Tebow to play.

The Broncos went 1-2 in those three games, and afterward, management quickly went to work. Bowlen's first move was to formally hire Elway to run the football operations, three days after the nightmarish season ended.

A week later, on Jan. 13, 2011, Elway, Xanders and Bowlen made Fox – the anti-Josh in terms of age, experience and personality – the 14th head coach in franchise history.

From Day One, Elway and Fox had to deal with the Orton-Tebow quarterback controversy they inherited.

Both Elway and Fox regarded Orton as a decent NFL quarterback. They didn't know what to think of Tebow, good or bad. There was no question where Xanders stood on the issue, though. He liked what he saw from Tebow in his three-game audition at season's end.

In his first NFL start, at Oakland, Tebow became only the second

PAT BOWLEN TURNED TO THE ICON, JOHN ELWAY, TO RIGHT THE SHIP. *John Leyba, The Denver Post*

> "When you play this position, there's always something going on. **I'm here.** My mind-set is I'm going to be here. I've let the team know I want to be here. I plan on playing my best ball."
>
> **Kyle Orton,** the Broncos' starting quarterback

NFL quarterback to have a rushing touchdown of at least 40 yards and a passing touchdown of at least 30 yards in the same game. He did both in the first quarter.

In his second start, Tebow helped the Broncos overcome a 17-0 halftime deficit against Houston by passing for 308 yards and a touchdown, and running for another score in a 24-23 comeback win. It was the first of Tebow's patented fourth-quarter comebacks; the Broncos trailed 23-10 entering the final 15 minutes.

In his third and last game as a rookie, at home against San Diego, Tebow's passing flaws were exposed. He completed 16-of-36 passes with two interceptions. But again he displayed his uncommon competitive fire by nearly leading the Broncos back from a 26-7 deficit late in the third quarter. Tebow threw for one touchdown and ran for another to bring the Broncos to within 33-28, then had two Hail Mary passes to the end zone batted down on the game's final plays.

Xanders had seen enough.

He believed Tebow deserved to at least get the chance to lead the Broncos in 2011. Most notably, Xanders believed Tebow raised the level of play of his teammates. Whether through Tebow's gladiatorial style or his determined will when victory seemed hopeless, Xanders believed the Broncos' defense played better when Tebow was the quarterback. He also believed the offensive linemen blocked better, although they remained far more loyal to the veteran Orton.

Sure, Tebow would have growing pains as a passer in 2011. But as he developed and continued to improve, Xanders believed Tebow could figure out how to win some games the team might otherwise lose.

While Xanders believed it was better for the long-term good of the organization to find out sooner rather than later whether Tebow could make it as a starting-caliber NFL quarterback – and by starting-caliber, the Broncos mean Super Bowl-caliber – the general manager also believed it was important to trade Orton.

The general manager's No. 1 task is to put together the best possible 53-man roster that fits within the guidelines of the salary cap. Orton's $8.8 million salary in 2011 was too much money for a backup, especially one eligible for free agency at season's end.

And, as a guy who had established himself as a starting quarterback, Orton did not figure to embrace the role of holding Tebow's baseball cap.

The desire of both Orton to play elsewhere and Xanders to move him led to considerable internal discussion during the offseason before Elway, Fox and everyone else inside Broncos headquarters agreed on a plan. Orton would be traded. Tebow would get his chance.

If Fox wasn't comfortable with how Tebow was running his offense in training camp, he could always count on Brady Quinn, a first-round pick by Cleveland in 2007 and a 12-game starter in 2008-09, to stopgap the quarterback position.

Then Miami backed down and the Broncos' plan fell apart. The Broncos didn't want the Dolphins to know it at the time, but they would have taken a bag of footballs in return for Orton. They just wanted to move his salary and and start the Tebow era.

When the Broncos officially began training camp on Thursday, July 28, there would be another twist to the Orton-Tebow saga: Orton outplayed Tebow by a wide margin.

As The Denver Post reported:

As arguably the biggest celebrity Denver has ever had, Elway understands that what Orton has gone through the past week isn't ideal. But as the Broncos' new football operations boss and former star quarterback, Elway also wasn't surprised to watch Orton perform coolly and efficiently in the opening workout of training camp Thursday.

"You hate to see anybody go through that, but the bottom line is the best players will play," Elway said. "There's always going to be pressure with that position, whether they're the expectations of being the first pick of the draft or expectations that are passed down. It doesn't matter who's under center, there's going

TEBOW HAD NEVER BEEN A THIRD-STRINGER. SOME QUESTIONED WHETHER HE WAS FOURTH BEST. *John Leyba, The Denver Post*

to be great expectations. It's a tough job and there are tough situations."

Orton not only remains the starter, the first day of training camp revealed that No. 2 quarterback Tebow must improve in a hurry if he's going to give the incumbent much competition.

Orton was his usual polished self. The design of every NFL pass play is that there will always be one receiver open. Maybe not two, but always one. Orton seemed to almost nonchalantly spot the open receiver every time, and his passes were precise. The Orton-to-Brandon Lloyd connections picked up where they left off in 2010.

Tebow got just as many reps but didn't seem to see the field the same way. He was a tick slower in finding the open receiver.

To be fair, it's probably unfair to compare Orton, who has been a four-season NFL starter, with Tebow, who has started just three games.

"We've got to work on some timing with certain things, but for a first day, I thought it was pretty good," Tebow said.

Orton's closest competitor Thursday was Quinn, who seemed to play with greater ease and confidence compared with his play in last year's camp.

Quinn had the first day's best line. Asked if there was any tension between Orton and Tebow, Quinn said: "Look, if you're going to ask questions about football, ask questions about football. I'm not here to talk about anyone's relationship status.

Save that for Twitter or Facebook or some message board."

"I've said this before: When you play this position, there's always something going on," Orton said. "I'm here. My mind-set is I'm going to be here. I've let the team know I want to be here. I plan on playing my best ball."

• • •

Orton was quarterbacking very well through the training camp sessions, while Tebow seemed to press. It wouldn't be accurate to say he was in denial when he was asked to describe his first training camp practice of the season.

It's just that Tebow sees his play differently from how impartial observers might see it. People who have watched NFL quarterbacks pass in practice for years – people such as Elway, Fox and Xanders – do not see passes wobble so noticeably or miss so badly.

The unflattering first-practice account in The Denver Post began to mushroom. Radio talk-show hosts seized on it. More and more stories with negative slants on Tebow's training camp struggles circulated.

And, no matter how much Tebow tried to insulate himself, criticism has a way of always finding its intended target. One week into training camp, and one week before the Broncos would play their first preseason game at Dallas, Denver Post columnist Woody Paige caught up with Tebow in a private moment.

Wrote Paige:

For the first time in more than a dozen conversations we have had, Tebow revealed edginess, frustration and even anger. Perhaps, now, nine days from his 24th birthday, Tebow is coming to grips with the reality of pro football and manhood. An All-American young man's life generally, and recently, had been rainbows and unicorns with trophies, championships, millions of dollars, adulation, an autobiography, commercial endorsements and an idyllic family and home.

On Wednesday, July 27, the Broncos were negotiating with the Dolphins on a trade of Kyle Orton, and the assumption was that Tebow would be the starting quarterback in Denver once Orton was moved.

Now, the Broncos appear to have decided that Orton will be their starter this season, and Tebow, according to an eruption locally and nationally, is as big a bust as the Cherry Creek gold field.

Tebow acknowledged in an interview Wednesday evening that the abrupt change in events affected him mentally and, possibly in one practice, physically.

"I didn't have a good day on the field (last) Saturday, but I think in the other practices, I've thrown well and improved each day," he said.

On Wednesday, former NFL running back and current ESPN analyst Merril Hoge unleashed a series of tweets basically condemning Tebow's ability. "It's embarrassing to think the Broncos could win with Tebow" … "College credentials do not translate to NFL … rare rare (sic) speeches do not work! You must poses (sic) a skill set to play! Tebow struggle with accuracy" … "That throwing motion he changed. You can't change who u r."

An hour after our talk, Tebow posted his own tweet: "Hey Merril … 'ppreciate that."

"I'm trying to insulate myself from what people in the media are saying," Tebow said. "But I've seen some of it, and it hurts because it's coming from people who haven't seen me practice, haven't seen me play, haven't seen what I can do. I did an interview the other day with someone on the NFL Network who said last year I'd never play a down in the NFL. He was wrong.

"Others who say I won't make it are wrong. They don't know what I'm capable of and what's inside me. My family and my friends have been bothered by what's gone on, and I tell them to pay no attention to it. I'm relying as always on my faith. …

"I know that all this (controversy) will have a way of working out."

• • •

Tebow would be proved prophetic, but it would take a while.

> "Others who say I won't make it are wrong. They don't know what I'm capable of and what's inside me. My family and my friends have been bothered by what's gone on, and I tell them to pay no attention to it. **I'm relying as always on my faith.**"
>
> — Tim Tebow

ORTON WAS GETTING THE REPUTATION AS A QB WHO COULDN'T DELIVER IN CRUNCH TIME. *John Leyba, The Denver Post*

WILL TO WIN: CHAPTER 2

FOX LIKED TEBOW'S "INTANGIBLES." BUT IT WASN'T UNTIL WEEK 5 THAT TEBOW WOULD GET HIS SHOT. *John Leyba, The Denver Post*

Orton played well in the preseason. The Broncos' first-teamers played well in the preseason. In the first test at Dallas, Orton and the first-string offense had one drive. They started at their own 20, and 10 plays later they reached first-and-goal at the 1. They couldn't punch it in, but all in all, Orton's effort was encouraging.

Tebow came in and would have had an interception except for a pass interference call. He recovered to complete 6-of-7 passes for 91 yards, but he essentially produced only one field goal in 1½ quarters. (An interception set up another Denver field goal as the offense got the ball at Dallas' 7.)

Quinn, the No. 3 quarterback, had the best performance. He completed 8-of-14 for 120 yards and a touchdown. He also directed the Broncos on another fourth-quarter march. At that point, it seemed Tebow was doomed. His chance to become the starting quarterback was never worse than in the week leading up to preseason game No. 2.

Quinn had earned his promotion to Orton's backup. Tebow was No. 3, although Fox refused to announce his new No. 2 QB.

Then came the second preseason game, and all it did was further bury Tebow. Orton was splendid, completing 10-of-13 for 135 yards, with a 135.1 passer rating. When he was given the rest of the night off halfway through the second quarter, the Broncos were up on the Bills 14-3. Quinn played well while completing the second quarter and leading the Broncos to 10 points in the third quarter. He was 10-of-16 for 130 yards and a touchdown.

Tebow? By the time he went in with 10:59 left in the game, the Broncos were ahead by two touchdowns. He got two possessions and completed 1-of-2 passes for 10 yards. His primary job was to run out the clock, which meant handing the ball off.

Tebow had overcome adversity throughout his life, but he had never been a third-stringer before. This was rough.

"I guess from the outside looking at it, as a competitor, it can be a little frustrating," Tebow said. "But I believe that when we actually play a real football game, I can play the game of football."

In the week leading up to the Broncos' third preseason game, against

Seattle, media commentary began crossing the line from critique to maliciousness.

Hoge and former NFL quarterback Boomer Esiason regurgitated year-old criticisms of Tebow's throwing mechanics.

"He can't play. He can't throw," Esiason told USA Today in its Aug. 23 edition, three days after the Buffalo preseason game. "I'm not here to insult him."

No? Boomer is an intelligent football analyst. But he obviously had not looked up the definition of "insult." Esiason was on a roll with the national newspaper. He couldn't stop himself from delivering the common cheap shot that has been flung at Tebow since he became a young adult.

"Just because he's God-fearing and a great person off the field and was a winner with a (Florida) team that had the best athletes in college football doesn't mean his game is going to translate to the NFL," Esiason said.

"What Josh McDaniels saw in him God only knows. Maybe God does know – because the rest of us don't."

Good one, Boomer.

In the same article, former Broncos quarterback and NFL analyst Steve Beuerlein said, "I'd say he's closer to a third-teamer than a first-teamer."

Beuerlein should know one from the other. He was a quintessential second-teamer.

Hoge, who often ripped Tebow's "elongated throwing motion," made the leap to a personal attack when he texted: "It's embarrassing to think the Broncos could win with Tebow." (During the season, Hoge must have turned several shades of red when the Tebow-led Broncos went on a 7-1 run.)

But the most spiteful take on Tebow between preseason game No. 2 against Buffalo and No. 3 against Seattle was delivered anonymously in a Yahoo.com report: A "highly knowledgeable member of the organization" said that given a fair competition, Tebow would be the No. 4 quarterback behind not only Kyle Orton and Brady Quinn, but undrafted rookie Adam Weber.

When asked about the anonymous leak, Fox scoffed, "It could have been the chef."

Against the Seahawks, Tebow not only earned some redemption, he delivered a precursor to the regular season by leading the Broncos on a game-winning drive that ended with 0:00 remaining.

The only problem was no one thought it meant much. In fact, it was dismissed as insignificant because Orton left the game in the third quarter with a 17-3 lead.

Because Tebow had played much less than Quinn in the first two preseason games, he went in after Orton finished his work in Game 3. In his only third-quarter series, Tebow completed a 20-yard dart to rookie tight end Julius Thomas, then went to work in the fourth quarter.

Read that before? Tebow threw a nice pass down the right sideline to backup running Jeremiah Johnson for a 23-yard gain to set up a field goal.

With 1:12 remaining, the score was 20-20 and the Broncos had the ball at their own 23. A long way to go with not much time. Tebow Time. On the first play, Tebow scrambled for 19 yards. A pass to the left flat found Lance Ball, who turned it into a 26-yard gain. Two plays and the Broncos were in field-goal range. Steven Hauschka connected from 51 yards to end the game.

Tebow's late-game effort didn't improve his depth-chart position. He went back to third-string. Although Fox never did say who his No. 2 QB was behind Orton, it was obvious for preseason game No. 4 at Arizona that it was Quinn, who got the start and played the entire first half. That left the second half for Tebow and Weber to split. All Quinn needed was a mediocre performance in the preseason finale and Tebow might never have seen the field in 2011.

Instead, Quinn was worse than mediocre with the second-team offense. He fumbled on a sack that put Arizona in field-goal position. He threw an interception that set up another Cardinals field goal. In all, he completed 4-of-12 passes for 26 yards. That computed to a 7.6 passer rating. Ouch.

Finally, Tebow had a chance. A small chance, and only for the No. 2 spot. But a chance.

And he delivered. As usual, it took him a while. It was 26-0 Arizona when Tebow got the ball at his own 6-yard line with 4:33 remaining.

Most likely, it would be Tebow's last drive of the preseason. With Orton scheduled to open as the starter,

> "I prefer a gamer to a good practice player. ... I want someone who will execute under pressure in a game."
> Coach **John Fox** on the Broncos' starting quarterback

WILL TO WIN: CHAPTER 2

QUINN HAD A TOUGH OUTING AGAINST ARIZONA IN THE FINAL PRESEASON GAME, OPENING THE DOOR FOR TEBOW TO CAPTURE THE BACKUP QUARTERBACK JOB HEADING INTO THE REGULAR SEASON. *Paul Connors, The Associated Press*

it might have been the last time Tebow would lead a full drive, for all anyone knew. After all, the plan was this: Orton plays well. Orton stays healthy. Orton leads the Broncos to enough wins to make the playoffs.

"Absolutely a fair statement," Tebow said at season's end. "You never know what's going to happen. NFL – Not For Long."

It was not an overstatement that this late, fourth-quarter series against the Cardinals would be a make-or-break drive for Tebow.

He answered by doing something he had never done before – he never left the pocket. He didn't watch the pass rush, didn't think about scrambling. He took the shotgun snap and kept his eyes downfield on his receivers.

It's almost as if offensive coordinator Mike McCoy told Tebow: Just this once, don't take off running, stay in the pocket and throw.

"No. It just worked out that way," Tebow said after the season. "I remember thinking after the first play, this isn't the time to try to get first downs or score. It's time to show I could go through my progressions."

First play, Tebow hit D'Andre Goodwin for 13 yards. Ball at the Broncos' 19. Next play, Tebow threw a beautiful touch pass down the right sideline, dropping the ball just over a cornerback into Goodwin's hands for a 26-yard gain. The ball was at the Denver 45. Two short passes to running back Jeremiah Johnson produced an incompletion and no gain. Third-and-10 at his own 45. Tebow connected with Eron Riley for 12 yards.

Now the ball was at the Arizona 43. Tebow dropped back from the shotgun and threw a beautiful deep ball down the right sideline to Riley, who was open from Phoenix to Denver.

Touchdown. Tebow was 5-of-6 on the drive for all 94 yards. It was by far the best he had looked as a passer in his year and a half with the Broncos.

Afterward, it was dismissed by the media as Tebow passing against second- and third-teamers. But there were second- and third-teamers on his side, too.

In the first significant decision of the John Fox-John Elway regime, Orton was officially named the Broncos' starting quarterback. For Tebow, it would be nearly six more weeks before he would throw another pass in an NFL game.

"I'm a believer that you do the best you can while making the best decisions, and things will work out the way they should," Elway would say in early December.

"At that point, with what Fix saw in training camp, Kyle was the more ready quarterback."

In hindsight, Fox may have gone against his first instinct. In an interview with Denver Post columnist Woody Paige in early July, when the lockout was still threatening the start of the season, Fox said: "I prefer a gamer to a good practice player. ... I want someone who will execute under pressure in a game."

Before season's end, it was startling how Orton proved to be an impressive practice player but failed to come through with the game on the line in the fourth quarter.

Tebow, meanwhile, may be the NFL's worst practice player. He also may be, given the deficiencies in footwork and throwing motion, the league's No. 1 gamer. No other player in the NFL plays leaps and bounds better in the clutch than he does in other moments of a game.

"I knew the intangibles that kid had," Fox said while looking back in early December. "I had a guy like that for a lot of years in Carolina with Jake (Delhomme). Jake wasn't

WHEN HE GOT HIS CHANCE, TEBOW STAYED IN THE POCKET AND PUT ON AN IMPRESSIVE DISPLAY. *Christian Petersen, Getty Images*

pretty. He wasn't that prototypical quarterback. But he was a winner. Those intangibles are huge."

It would take a while, though, for Fox to give Tebow a legit chance.

After the Broncos lost a heartbreaker at Tennessee to fall to 1-2 in the regular season – and with the powerhouse Green Bay Packers up next – Elway told Fox to start giving Tebow some reps in practice.

"We've got to see what we've got in Tebow," Elway told Fox. "We need to get him some reps because Kyle is taking everything. The last thing you want to do is put Tebow out there and not have him be ready."

Orton started the first five games of the regular season. With the 1-3 Broncos trailing San Diego 23-10 at halftime of Game 5, and Orton seemingly losing confidence by the week, Fox made the move.

Tebow was in.

"That surprised me because that was a little earlier than I thought it was going to be," Elway said later.

Those who knew Tebow from an early age would not have been surprised.

HE WAS THE COMEBACK KID, DETERMINED TO PLAY QUARTERBACK

When Tim Tebow was 11 years old, going on 12, he was doing 400 push-ups and 400 sit-ups a day.

Every day.

Why was an underdeveloped 11-year-old doing 400 push-ups and 400 sit-ups a day?

Because his father would not allow Tim to lift weights. Not until he reached puberty. Bob Tebow used to preach the workout habits of Herschel Walker to his youngest son. When Walker was considered the best college running back in the nation at Georgia, his workout routine became legendary, both for its volume and simplicity.

Walker never lifted weights. At age 12, though, he was doing 300 push-ups and 300 sit-ups a day. Think it's a coincidence that Tim Tebow settled on 400 and 400 for his daily routine?

"But I would get so sore," Tebow said. "Finally, I went to my dad and told him how sore I was getting. He asked me, 'How often are you doing them?' I told him, 'Every day.' He said, 'Every day? You're not supposed to do them every day.' I got smarter about it. I finally learned you actually get more out of it if you don't do them every day and let your muscles recover."

By the time Tim was 14, his father gave in. Tim's older brothers, Robby and Peter, were lifting weights, and Tim figured he needed to get stronger to keep up.

At age 14 and weighing about 175 pounds in the summer between eighth grade

TIM TEBOW DIDN'T COME BY HIS STURDY, MUSCULAR PHYSIQUE ACCIDENTALLY. *John Leyba, Denver Post*

and his freshman year of high school, the home-schooled Tebow did 315 curl reps of a 55-pound bar. It's not an exaggeration to say the lactic acid buildup would not allow him to straighten his arms for three days.

Why did Tebow do 55-pound curls 315 times in one set? Because it was a summer-camp contest. He was the next-to-last contestant. When it was his turn, the rep number to beat was 55. Tebow didn't stop at 56 because the guy behind him, the last guy in line, was big. Really big.

So Tebow wanted to do all he could to post a number difficult to approach. The big guy didn't come close.

Another story. When Tebow arrived at the University of Florida, he showed up early. He should have been finishing his senior year of high school, but thanks in part to the flexibility of home schooling, he was able to get his diploma a semester early.

He attended Florida in the spring semester of 2006 so he could get a jump on other incoming freshmen by playing spring ball. A month into conditioning, the team was holding regular tug-of-war contests.

One morning, Tebow was matched against a defensive tackle. There was no line on either side that marked victory. Victory came only when one contestant conceded.

Tebow pulled the defensive tackle across the weight room. No concession. He pulled the defensive tackle into the men's bathroom. No concession.

He pulled the defensive tackle – remember, Tebow was not only a quarterback, but a quarterback who had not yet started his freshman season – to a stall door and kicked it open. He started yanking the defensive tackle into the stall when the conditioning coach, Mick Marotti, blew his whistle to mercifully end the drill.

PAM TEBOW'S DOCTOR TOLD HER THAT "AN ABORTION IS THE ONLY WAY TO SAVE YOUR LIFE." THE FAMILY PRAYED.
Special to The Denver Post

Tim Tebow grew up obsessive about winning and compulsive about becoming the best he could be.

People wonder, where did all those unlikely fourth-quarter comebacks come from? They were there from birth. Tebow has been pulling out victories from the day he was born.

Devoted Tebow fans are familiar with the story. Bob Tebow, a Baptist pastor in Florida, and his wife Pam felt the call to be missionaries in the Philippines because of their affection for the large population of orphan children in the island nation. The family – which included daughters Christy and Katie and sons Robby and Peter – moved there in 1985.

The Tebows didn't settle in the large, more civilized cities such as Manila, the nation's capital, or Davao, at least not initially. They took shelter in General Santos City in the primitive southern island of Mindanao.

Early in Pam Tebow's fifth pregnancy, she experienced extreme pain and heavy bleeding, and a Mindanao doctor recommended an abortion. The doctor said there was a distinct possibility Pam Tebow would not survive childbirth if she went through with the delivery.

"An abortion is the only way to save your life," the doctor told Pam Tebow, according to Tim Tebow's autobiography.

The Tebows prayed. Prayed hard. Prayed constantly. God, they said, led them to seek a second opinion, this time in Manila, where the Tebows consulted with an American-trained doctor. Later in Pam's pregnancy, the bleeding subsided. Because Pam needed regular medical attention, the family moved to Manila.

Timothy Richard Tebow was delivered barely attached to his placenta on Aug. 14, 1987, in the Makati City Medical Center. Timothy, which means "honoring God," had to stay in the hospital a week because he was losing weight and his mom needed surgery.

More prayers. Both recovered.

On Christmas Day 2011, after returning to Denver from a disappointing Christmas Eve loss at Buffalo, Tebow got to see himself from his toddler days in the Philippines.

"My mom brought us all these home videos I had never seen before," Tebow said. "It has me at 2 years old running around, and my brothers were way bigger than I was, and Robby is just crushing me. I was running on the field holding a football and a baseball, and Robby is decked out in this full Dallas Cowboys uniform and Peter is running around with this half-cracked helmet, and I'm running around just getting killed. In every video, I'm playing with some type of ball. I'm always playing."

The Tebows lived in Manila until Tim was 3, when they moved back

AN ALL-AROUND ATHLETE, TEBOW'S STRONGEST SPORT IN HIGH SCHOOL WAS BASEBALL. *Gary Wilcox, Orlando Sentinel*

Gary Wilcox, Orlando Sentinel

Diane Stover, Orlando Sentinel

TEBOW (BACK ROW, FAR RIGHT) GOT TO PLAY QUARTERBACK IN HIS FOURTH YEAR OF POP WARNER. *Courtesy of the Orlando Sentinel*

to Jacksonville, Fla. When Tim was 5, Bob Tebow got the bright idea of moving the family to a farm.

"It was such a blessing," Tebow said. "We got it at a government auction. It was a great place to have five kids grow up and work. I think that built as much character in us as anything else."

Daily chores for the Tebow boys included keeping up with the horses, tossing around bales of hay, chopping wood and feeding the cows.

"My dad would leave the country, and first it was Robby's responsibility to take care of the farm, but by the time I was 11 or 12, everybody would leave for five weeks in the summer to go to the Philippines," Tebow said. "And it would just be me and my mom at the house because I was too young to go. So it was my responsibility until I was old enough to go (at age 15) to care of the cows, take care of the horses, take care of the chickens, take care of our garden, cut the grass."

The garden was no backyard variety. It was huge and contained corn, squash, zucchini, cucumbers and okra.

"It was way too big," Tebow said. "My dad did it for misery. It was like a half-acre garden. It was ridiculous to work in that."

Tim played sports every day with his two older brothers on the farm. Baseball in the summer. Football in the fall. Basketball in winter.

The truth: For most of his youth, Tim was more naturally gifted at baseball than any other sport. A left-handed slugger, he won his share of the annual Home Run Derbys his league sponsored. Tim "The Bambino" Tebow.

TEBOW TRANSFERRED TO NEASE HIGH WHERE HE COULD PLAY QUARTERBACK – AND WIN A STATE TITLE. *Gary Wilcox, Orlando Sentinel*

WILL TO WIN: CHAPTER 3

It was while playing baseball that Tebow came up with his throwing motion that would later become the most discussed delivery since Paul Revere warned of the British.

"That's 100 percent pitching," he said.

Tebow then pantomimed a pitch from the rubber, lifting his front knee, dropping his arm back.

"The coaches taught me that you break and you separate and you drop and then you follow through," Tebow said, demonstrating as he talked. "And that's what I did first before I starting playing football. I pitched and developed my natural throwing motion."

Too bad he wasn't a catcher, where the delivery is cocked no further than the ear hole — the same motion as a quarterback. Peyton Manning's passing technique is not unlike that of a baseball catcher.

"Yeah, but I'm left-handed," Tebow said. "Everything I did in baseball was elongated because I was a pitcher, I was a first baseman and I played the outfield."

• • •

Tim Tebow is dyslexic. The learning disorder runs in his family. His dad is dyslexic and so is Robby, who is 6 years older. All three are kinesthetic learners, which means they learn best by doing.

"If you say let's figure out how to work this TV," Tebow said, "well, if you tell me, 'Hit this, this and this,' I won't remember it as well. But if I go through it and do it, then I'll have it."

Could this help explain why Tebow grew up to perform considerably better in games than practice?

"I just think in games it's a fight," he said. "And you do whatever you can to get past that line. Practice is, it's about learning and improving. The game is not thinking almost, it's playing, it's what you do in the backyard with your brothers."

Pam Tebow helped her sons understand that dyslexia has nothing to do with intelligence. Bob Tebow has an extremely high IQ.

It just meant the Tebow men had to process learning differently from others.

"I don't think it's a handicap at all for me," Tebow said. "It's something where the education program for this interests me. There's not a cookie-cutter way of, 'Hey, this is how it is and based on these tests, this is your intelligence level.' No, that's silly. Some kids are brilliant in different ways."

All the Tebow children were homeschooled by their mom – one-on-one instruction where homework assignments were heavy. Dinner at the kitchen table often came with quizzes on the state and world capitals, U.S. presidents and Bible verses.

Contrary to perception, homeschooled children do not necessarily lack social interaction. Tim had plenty of friends through church and sports and said home schooling enabled him to interact better with adults. Because he wasn't around a classroom full of kids, in many ways he didn't act like a kid. He was often around adults. In social settings, adults know how to be polite and can demonstrate manners, at least more than kids.

To this day, Tebow often begins his conversations with people he is just meeting with, "Yes, sir" and "Yes, ma'am."

This will surprise no one familiar with Tebow's story, but from the time he started playing Pop Warner football, he had trouble convincing his coaches he was a quarterback.

In his first organized football game, he played running back, much to his dismay. He did get to play quarterback, but as he moved up to the peewee league, his coach said he was thinking of making Tim a fullback.

"OK," Tebow's dad replied. "I'm thinking about having Timmy play for another team."

When it was time to pick a high school for athletics, the choice was a no-brainer. Tim would play for Jacksonville Trinity Christian Academy. Robby and Peter played there, and Tim would, too. In Tim's freshman year, though, Trinity coach Verlon Dorminey insisted the younger Tebow play linebacker, just like his brothers.

"He's too athletic to play quarterback," Dorminey told Bob Tebow.

Duh! After Tim's freshman year, the Tebows went looking for another high school where a coach would let him play quarterback. He landed at Nease High, a public school.

Imagine, then, what the Tebows felt a few years later when he was about to enter the NFL draft and analysts such as former Dallas Cowboys coach Jimmy Johnson said he might make a better H-back (small tight end), while others said he should play fullback, running back or linebacker.

The Jimmy Johnsons of the world would have understood the silliness of such notions had they known

> "I didn't mind jokes about going to school in my pajamas, **but I didn't want anyone to say I was soft.**"
> **Tim Tebow** recounting a run-in over his home-schooling

TEBOW PICKED FLORIDA OVER ALABAMA AND WOULD WIN A HEISMAN TROPHY AND TWO NATIONAL TITLES. *Phil Sandlin, The Associated Press*

Tebow's background. Playing a position other than quarterback is not an option. Never has been for Tebow. Never will be.

In selecting Nease, Tebow didn't exactly pick a high school powerhouse. Put it this way: In his first football season at the school, his sophomore year, Nease played in six homecoming games.

By now, people know Tebow enough to realize he wasn't playing football for the fun of it or to be somebody's homecoming pushover.

He might have been the new kid in school, but that didn't stop him from pushing his teammates to excel. In one case, literally.

Tim had just jumped on his receivers for being "lackadaisical." One of the receivers shot back with: "Pretty big word for a homeschooler." Tim pushed the kid. As in two-handed shove.

"I'm still friends with him," Tebow said when reminded of the story.

There is a perception Christians can be timid, even soft. Tebow lowers his shoulder pads into such a stereotype.

"It's so the opposite. At least it should be," he said. "That sometimes bothers me when people say that Christians are always soft. As a Christian, you should be kind and turn the other cheek, but at the same time you need to be the toughest one, you need to be the one setting an example, you need to show character, you need to be the one working hard."

It's difficult to pinpoint exactly why Tebow became such a phenomenon.

THE DENVER POST 35

| | | | | WILL TO WIN: CHAPTER 3 | | | | |

TEBOW AND FLORIDA TEAMMATES SUFFERED A 32-13 LOSS TO ALABAMA IN THE SEC CHAMPIONSHIP HIS SENIOR YEAR, RUINING A SHOT AT ANOTHER NATIONAL TITLE. *John Amis, The Associated Press*

Probably because there is not one reason but many. It's less difficult zeroing in on when it all started, at least on a national scale. Between his junior and senior year, ESPN broadcast a documentary on Tebow entitled, "The Chosen One."

It's a remarkably inspiring piece that shows the teenager as a leader, and sometimes gung-ho competitor, who was the same person then as he is now.

The attention didn't affect him as he led Nease to the Class 4A state championship in his senior season. In the title game, Tebow passed for four touchdowns and ran for two, a Florida state championship record.

In heavy demand by Division I football recruiters, Tebow took unofficial and official visits to Alabama, LSU, Florida State, Miami, Ohio State, Michigan, USC, Notre Dame and Florida. He quickly crossed the Fighting Irish off his list because it was bone-chilling cold the day he saw Notre Dame play in South Bend, Ind.

USC didn't have much of a chance because it was too far away from home and family. Georgia crossed Tebow off its list after it received a commitment from Matthew Stafford. In the end, Tebow's decision came down to two schools: Alabama, whose coach was Mike Shula, and Florida, led by Urban Meyer and his spread offense.

After leading Nease to the state championship, Tebow had two days to decide. ESPN would be carrying his decision during a news conference on Dec. 13. On the morning of the decision, Alabama and Florida remained tied for first.

"That definitely was the hardest decision I ever made in my life," Tebow said in a recent interview. "I was agonizing, sweating. It was a miserable time. It was supposed to be a great day for me. It was one of the worst."

Tebow prayed for the Lord to help him determine where to play, but in his mind and heart, the answer remained elusive.

Thirty minutes before Tebow's news conference to announce the college program of his choice, he was still conflicted. Finally, he went to his dad, who asked, "Who's the one person you want to play for?"

After choosing, he placed his first call to Shula.

"I told him I was going to Florida, and he could tell I was crying because I thought I was going to Alabama since I was a freshman," Tebow said. "I loved the passion of Alabama because I felt like that was my passion. And the coaches, and the hugs and the sweet tea, and the people – it felt like home to me.

"But then Urban, his passion and love for the game and the way he believed in me and I was thinking: There's something special with him."

So he calls Shula and he's crying as he says he's going to Florida.

"And he says, 'Stop crying, stop crying,' " Tebow said. " 'I love you just as much now as if you came to Alabama. You're going to have a great career, and hopefully I'm going to be able to coach you one day.' And I hung up with him and I looked at Dad and said, 'That's the coach I want to play for!' "

For the next week, Tebow had no peace with his decision.

Tebow's freshman year at Florida

WHILE TEBOW'S FATHER AND BROTHERS WERE OFF IN THE PHILIPPINES, HE STAYED WITH HIS MOTHER, PAM. *Special to The Denver Post*

brought the jump pass and a national championship. His sophomore season brought the Heisman Trophy. His junior year brought "The Promise" and another national championship. His senior year brought a bachelor's degree in family, youth and community sciences and capped arguably the greatest college football career of all time, with 88 touchdown passes and 57 touchdown runs.

And, on April 22, 2010, the Broncos traded three draft picks – selections in the second, third and fourth rounds – to the Baltimore Ravens in exchange for their No. 25 overall pick in the first round.

NFL commissioner Roger Goodell walked to center stage at Radio City Music Hall in downtown Manhattan.

"With the 25th pick in the 2010 NFL draft, the Denver Broncos select Tim Tebow, quarterback, Florida."

The next day, Tebow was introduced to the Denver media at Broncos headquarters.

Wrote Lindsay H. Jones of The Denver Post:

The tall tales of Tebow's high school and collegiate feats are true, not fiction.

Tebow once played three quarters of a prep game – and scored on a 29-yard run – with a broken leg. (He missed the rest of that season.) In his final game at Nease High School in Ponte Vedra, Fla., he begged his way off the sideline and into the Panthers' defensive line, where he lined up at nose guard on the final series of the game. (His team won.) At Florida, he became the first sophomore to win the Heisman Trophy after one of the best statistical seasons in college football history: 3,286 yards passing, 895 yards rushing and 55 total touchdowns. He was on two Southeastern Conference and two national championship teams – one each as a role player and one each as the Gators' star. In his final game with the Gators, he completed 31-of-35 passes for 482 yards and accounted for four touchdowns (three passing, one rushing) in the Sugar Bowl.

That's only part of the lore.

• • •

Where the legend of Tebow grew to Bunyanesque proportions, where his fame went beyond the Saturday afternoon crowd and crossed over to all fans of all sports, was when he delivered "The Promise."

The goal going into his junior season of 2008 was not just a national championship but an undefeated season, which Florida had never accomplished.

It looked like the goal the Gators would reach too, after starting 3-0 by routing Hawaii 56-10, dominating rival Miami 26-3 and destroying Tennessee 30-6 in Knoxville.

Game 4 figured to be another easy win as the Gators played a pedestrian Ole Miss (2-2) team at The Swamp, with the Rebels coming off a loss to Vanderbilt.

But for this one Saturday afternoon on Sept. 27, 2008, the game went Ole Miss' way, the Rebels pulling off a 31-30 stunner. Tebow was sensational in defeat, completing 24-of-38 for 319 yards and a touchdown with no picks. He also rushed for two touchdowns.

Afterward, he sat despondent in front of his locker for a good 45 minutes, not wanting to talk to the media, although he knew at some point he must. As he finally walked to the podium with a single microphone at its center, Tebow still didn't know what he wanted to say. Showered and wearing a black T-shirt, Tebow said:

"I just want to say one thing ... (deep breath) ... to the fans and everybody in Gator Nation, um, ... (another deep breath, Tebow licks his lips and is clearly fighting back tears as he nearly chokes on his next words) ... I'm sorry.

"I'm extremely sorry. We were hoping for an undefeated season. That was my goal. It's something Florida has never done here. But I promise you one thing, a lot of good will come out of this. ... (talking fast now, without a breath) ... You will never see any player in the entire country play as hard as I will play the rest of the season. And you will never have someone push the rest of the team as hard as I will push everybody the rest of the season, and you will never see a team play harder than we will the rest of this season. God bless."

It was so hokey. So corny. So Disney. And it was 100 percent authentic Tebow.

The next week, the Gators destroyed Arkansas in Fayetteville 38-7. LSU went down 51-21. Kentucky was obliterated 63-5. In the Georgia-Florida Football Classic that is played at the hardly neutral site of Jacksonville (Tebow's hometown), the Bulldogs had no chance, losing 49-10. Vandy was crushed 42-14. Steve Spurrier and South Carolina were trounced 56-6. The Citadel picked a bad time to accept a game at Florida, losing 70-19. Florida State got hammered 45-10.

In the SEC championship, No. 1 ranked Alabama couldn't keep up with Tebow. Florida rolled 31-20.

The national championship game pitted Tebow and the Florida Gators against Heisman Trophy winner Sam Bradford and the Oklahoma Sooners.

Poor Sam. Tebow threw for 231 yards and two touchdowns and ran for a season-high 109 yards on 22 carries in a 24-14 victory.

In the fourth quarter of the championship games against Alabama and Oklahoma, Tebow was 11-of-11 for 148 yards and two touchdowns. Tebow had made a promise and emphatically kept his word.

Had the Heisman Trophy election been conducted after the bowl games – as many argue it should – Tebow most likely would have won his second in a row.

As it was, he had his second national title and a speech that was immortalized.

Initially called by some "The Pledge," it later became universally known as "The Promise" throughout Gator Nation because the word was used in Tebow's postgame address. The Promise was later inscribed on a plaque and placed outside the front entrance of the Gators' new football facility at Ben Hill Griffin Stadium.

If it's not the most famous speech in college football history, it might be second to Knute Rockne's "Win one for the Gipper."

Notre Dame had to win only one game for George Gipp, albeit against undefeated Army.

Tebow had to win 10. Florida not only won those 10 games, it did so by an average margin of 33.8 points.

Tim Tebow was everybody's All-American. Tim Tebow had become a legend, one of the most recognizable athletes on the planet.

But could he make it in the NFL?

"THE PROMISE" WAS INSCRIBED ON A PLAQUE AND PLACED AT FLORIDA'S FOOTBALL FACILITY. *Andrew Stanfill, The Independent Florida Alligator*

"I promise you one thing, a lot of good will come out of this. You will never see any player in the entire country play as hard as I will play the rest of the season. And you will never have someone push the rest of the team as hard as I will push everybody the rest of the season, and you will never see a team play harder than we will the rest of this season. God bless."

Tim Tebow, in comments following Ole Miss' 31-30 upset of Florida

WILL TO WIN: CHAPTER 4

A GREAT COMPETITOR, A WINNER, A LEADER. BUT CAN HE PLAY IN THE PROS?

One of the greatest players in college football history was not going to make it in the NFL. Not at quarterback, he wasn't.

So said none other than Jimmy Johnson, the coach and architect of the great University of Miami teams in the 1980s and Dallas Cowboys teams in the 1990s and now an NFL analyst for Fox. Johnson was the first of the former coach/former player brigade to unleash dismissive opinions about Tebow's ability to play above the college level, where he dominated.

And make no mistake, college football has rarely seen the likes of Tebow. Heisman Trophy? He was the first sophomore to win it. He finished in the top-five voting two other times. National championships? He was part of two – first as a special-package force in his freshman season, and then as the unquestioned quarterback leader of the 2008 Florida Gators.

Statistics? He would not only rush for nearly 3,000 yards with 57 touchdowns – unheard-of totals for a quarterback – he was the second-highest-rated passer in college history, with an efficiency of 170.8 on 88 touchdown passes against 16 interceptions.

But, on the Dan Patrick radio show on Nov. 24, 2009, three days after Tebow played three quarters of Florida's 62-3 annihilation of Florida International, Johnson unleashed a verbal sledgehammer to Tebow's professional prospects.

"I don't think Tebow can play in a pro-style offense, not quarterback," Johnson said. "I think a team that's gonna look at Tim Tebow, they're gonna make one

TIM TEBOW DOMINATED IN COLLEGE. EXPERTS QUESTIONED WHETHER HE COULD CUT IT IN THE PROS. *Mark Humphrey, The Associated Press*

of two decisions. If they're going to bring him into their style of play, with their coaching staff, they've gotta project him to be maybe an H-back.

"I don't know if he's fast enough to be a receiver. Maybe he could be a tight end. I don't know if he can block, I don't know if he can catch the ball. But he's gotta play another position. He can't play quarterback."

Whoa. The harsh assessment by one of the most respected coaches in recent football history perked the ears of football fans and pundits nationwide. Tebow-bashing was off to the races. Within weeks, ripping Tebow's NFL prospects as a quarterback seemed to become a badge of honor.

With all due respect to Johnson – one of the best coaches, college or pro, to ever patrol the sidelines – he should have known Tebow had no intention of heeding his advice to work on his "get-off" technique in hopes of becoming an H-back.

Keep in mind, in his first year of peewee football, Tebow was told to play running back, even though he had asked his coach if he could play quarterback. The coach thought he was too big to play quarterback. (By the seventh grade, Tebow was doing 400 push-ups and 400 sit-ups a day. To say he was unusually strong by peewee standards would be an understatement.)

"Position by body stereotype" is how Tebow referred to the quarterback slight in his autobiography, "Through My Eyes."

What Johnson might not have realized is that Tebow switched high schools after his freshman year because his coach at Jacksonville Trinity Christian Academy insisted his body type and athleticism were better suited for him to play linebacker or tight end. (Tebow's two older brothers, Robby and Peter, played linebacker at Trinity. So in defense of the coach, it was an understandable decision.)

H-back, Jimmy Johnson? If Tebow can't play quarterback, he ain't playing football.

After Tebow led his team to victory in his first spring Orange and Blue scrimmage at the University of Florida, a couple of sportswriters covering the team stated his "style of play would never work in college football."

Tebow prevailed in that Florida spring scrimmage in what was supposed to be his final semester of high school. It was the flexibility of home schooling, and careful family planning, that allowed Tebow to start college a semester early. On purpose, Tebow made his decision on which college he would attend in mid-December rather than wait until national letter of intent signing day in early February. Tebow picked Urban Meyer and Florida ahead of Mike Shula and Alabama.

Tebow wanted to declare early so he could get a head start on playing spring ball, but also so he could help recruit undecided blue-chippers to Florida – players he had gotten to know through high school all-star games; stars such as Percy Harvin and Brandon Spikes, who wound up following Tebow to Florida.

So, at a time when other high school seniors were deciding on a college, Tebow was leading his Orange team past senior-to-be Chris Leak's Blue team. And, yes, already there were questions whether Tebow's style would translate to the highest-caliber college level that is the Southeastern Conference.

"I thought I silenced this debate from my freshman year of high school," Tebow wrote in his book.

He had never been more wrong.

The debate over Tebow's ability to play quarterback was just getting started.

Four days after Johnson questioned his ability to play the position in the NFL, Tebow led Florida to a 37-10 pasting of archrival Florida State, completing 17-of-21 passes for 221 yards, three touchdowns and no interceptions. He also rushed for 90 yards. In his next game, Tebow played well in defeat one final time at Florida. It was the SEC championship game, and No. 1 Florida was paired with No. 2 Alabama.

Tebow completed 20-of-35 passes for 247 yards and a touchdown and rushed 10 times for 63 yards. He threw a fourth-quarter pick in the end zone with his team down 32-13, which turned out to be the final score.

As the Gators' failed bid for a third national championship in four years ticked down, tears streamed down Tebow's face.

"He's a great player," said Alabama receiver Julio Jones, who later became a first-round draft pick of the Atlanta Falcons. "But man, we're tired of him."

Tebow would take a final bow. On Jan. 1, 2010, he led the Gators to a

> "He's gotta play another position.
> **He can't play quarterback.**"
> Jimmy Johnson, former college and NFL football coach

BEFORE LIGHTING UP FLORIDA STATE IN HIS SENIOR SEASON, TEBOW GREETS FANS DURING THE GATOR WALK. *Tom Burton, Orlando Sentinel*

51-24 whipping of Cincinnati in the Sugar Bowl. Tebow's final passing numbers? Get this: 31-of-35 for 482 yards, three touchdowns and no picks. His passer rating was 232.5, an almost unheard-of total even in the inflated college passer rating formula.

To Johnson's credit, he quickly softened his scouting report. Maybe he reconsidered after he was bombarded with irate sentiments from Tebow Nation. As anyone who has negatively assessed Tebow's play knows, to not openly cheerlead for Tebow is to draw the wrath of his fans.

Whatever the reason, by January 2010, Johnson had a more positive spin.

"The more I watch Tebow, the more I think he might be a (NFL) quarterback," Johnson said. "He has the arm strength. He makes accurate throws. He has the physical presence. He can get you believing."

The toothpaste was already out of the tube, though. Leading up to the NFL draft, Tebow critics were everywhere.

The intense scrutiny magnified during Senior Bowl week in late January, where the top college players eligible for the draft practice and play in Mobile, Ala. Every NFL team is represented by members of its coaching staff and personnel department. The top senior quarterbacks show off their skills.

And everybody was there to see if former Green Bay Packers quarterback Zeke Bratkowski had fixed Tebow's elongated release. Prior to his Senior Bowl audition, Tebow had spent two weeks with Bratkowski, who built a nice post-playing career as a renowned quarterbacks coach.

The Denver Post's Jeff Legwold attended the Senior Bowl practices in Mobile and reported on Tebow's mechanical issues when throwing.

"The biggest two of those are his footwork when he sets up to pass and his delivery," Legwold wrote. "Having played in the shotgun formation at Florida, Tebow rarely has been asked to work from behind center, to drop back three, five or seven steps as he scans a defense, and throw the ball on time."

• • •

Tebow struggled at the Senior Bowl practices, his first on-field audition for NFL coaches in a scaled-down version of a pro offense. Miami Dolphins coach Tony Sparano, whose staff coached the South team, gave him a lukewarm endorsement, saying Tebow's delivery was "fine" and that Florida's players were "well-

WILL TO WIN: CHAPTER 4

coached."

Tebow carries the ball low as he prepares to throw. He has a long arm swing on his delivery, much closer to a baseball pitch than the quick release required of NFL quarterbacks. Tebow tried to show he could deliver the ball more quickly in Mobile, but as he did so, his accuracy suffered.

"With the actual release, I think it's OK," Tebow said at the time. "I think there's definitely room for improvement in quickening it, absolutely."

Left unclear was whether his workouts had damaged Tebow to the point he would fall out of the first round of the NFL draft. For teams thinking they might take a flier on him and move him to another position, Tebow would have none of it. He would only play quarterback in the pros.

"You only need one team to believe," he said.

As it turned out, several NFL teams believed Tebow had a chance to make it as a quarterback and indicated they might choose him in the second or third rounds with the idea of grooming him.

Only the Broncos, though, proved willing to draft him in Round 1. Head coach Josh McDaniels and general manager Brian Xanders visited with Texas quarterback Colt McCoy on the Monday before the 2010 draft and with Tebow on Tuesday in Florida. McDaniels and Xanders came away far more impressed with Tebow.

The Broncos' first-round selection of Tebow, though, only heightened the scrutiny. Bashing the pick became almost a cottage industry.

ESPN analyst Trent Dilfer, a former Fresno State quarterback who was the No. 6 overall pick in the 1994 draft, was among the most prominent critics. Dilfer's first critique on Tebow came while filing a video report from the Senior Bowl.

"I said he doesn't have it mechanically," Dilfer said later. "I said his will is off the charts. I want to be wrong. But I did say this: You can never reach your athletic potential in any sport with flawed mechanics. Flawed mechanics is the limiting factor in reaching your athletic potential. It doesn't mean you can't be really good. But you can't be as good as you could be."

Mechanically, every scout knew Tebow had two major problems: his long release and his lousy footwork.

It didn't take a former quarterback, or coach for that matter, to see that the lefty had a delivery more suited to a right fielder uncorking a throw to the plate.

"I will be visibly biased toward Tim Tebow, hoping he succeeds because I'm one that said he won't," Dilfer said in an ESPN conference call with the national media prior to Tebow's NFL debut against the Jaguars in his hometown of Jacksonville. "I want to be wrong. I want Tim Tebow to be a superstar, because

> ## "Flawed mechanics is the limiting factor
> ### in reaching your athletic potential."
> **Trent Dilfer**, former NFL quarterback and studio analyst for ESPN

there's one thing you cannot coach and that's will. And I think he has the strongest will of any person we've seen in a long time."

Sounds good so far. But wait.

"Saying that, if he is successful as a quarterback in the first three years of his career, it will be one of the most remarkable jobs of coaching by Josh McDaniels and his staff that we have seen since the job Bill Walsh did with Joe Montana. It will be absolutely mind-boggling from a quarterback standpoint if Josh McDaniels and his staff can make him a successful quarterback in the first three years. Now, it wouldn't surprise me if five years from now he's successful."

Easy there, Trent, easy! One of the most remarkable jobs of coaching? Absolutely mind-boggling?

Greg Cosell, the nephew of former broadcast legend Howard Cosell and a longtime producer of NFL Films, was contacted by The New York Times for his assessment on Tebow entering the draft.

"On film, there is very little in Tebow's game that projects well at this point to the NFL," Cosell told The Times. "I could never draft a quarterback in the first round who does not show on tape the skill set and physical attributes that are demanded in the NFL.

"Number one, he has questionable and limited arm strength with a slow and ponderous delivery. Number two, in college he did not throw with timing or anticipation because the offense that he was in did not require it. In the NFL, there are certain throws in certain situations that necessitate that the ball is delivered before his receiver makes his break. He wasn't asked to do that at Florida.

"Thirdly, pocket movement in the NFL is far more important than running. Pocket movement is the ability to move within the confines of an area about the size of a boxing ring

TEBOW'S MECHANICAL BLEMISHES WERE UNDER A MICROSCOPE DURING SENIOR BOWL WEEK. *Phil Sandlin, The Associated Press*

WILL TO WIN: CHAPTER 4

while at the same time maintaining your downfield focus so you can deliver the football. Tebow did not exhibit that trait in college, probably because he was a runner. Nobody is a great NFL quarterback because of the way they run."

Many NFL scouts, coaches and general managers agreed with Cosell, even if they weren't the kind to use words such as ponderous.

Cosell's report left out Tebow's famed intangibles such as leadership, character, will to win, work ethic and love of the game.

Former Broncos coach Dan Reeves watched as reports of Tebow's struggles at the Senior Bowl and Pro Day workouts filtered in before the draft, and he felt his temperature rise. Reeves was an assistant in Dallas who coached Roger Staubach and was later the head coach in Denver and Atlanta, tutoring the likes of John Elway and Michael Vick. Those are only three of the most famous quarterbacks in NFL history.

Reeves told Denver Post columnist Woody Paige this past fall:

"When I watched that ESPN show last year about Tebow's workouts, it was like seeing Roger. Tebow's throwing technique is criticized. Roger carried the ball low too, because he was a scrambler and had to wind up to throw. He was a great passer. I've seen Tebow make the passes.

"The most important plays for quarterbacks are third downs and close to the goal. The coverage has to protect itself against quarterbacks who can run. They know (Kyle) Orton is going to stand in the pocket. Nobody knew what John was going to do.

"I'm not out there (at Broncos practices). I'm talking from a distance. But I know from experience that a guy like Tebow definitely makes a difference."

• • •

There was one negative evaluation in Cosell's report that many scouts disagree with. Tebow has a strong arm. It may take him a while to unload the ball, but Tebow throws a good deep ball. Don't let any former quarterback, Merril Hoge or passing guru say he doesn't.

And, on the intermediate passes, Tebow does throw with zip.

"He's got plenty of arm," said Elway, who had the strongest arm of them all. "When it's longer (in the delivery) like that, you have to anticipate a little bit more. He doesn't have confidence in that, yet. He'll get there."

Arm strength, though, is not measured by a radar gun alone. Yes, velocity is a measure of arm strength. But so is location, and Tebow is to accuracy what Peyton Manning is to mobility. Which is to say, not very good.

There are times when Tebow doesn't just miss with his passes, he's knock-over-the-water-cooler-on-the-bench wild. Tebow also throws a "heavy" ball, which receivers do not appreciate. His passes don't settle into a receiver's hands, as is the case with, yes, a Kyle Orton. Tebow's passes will thud into a receiver's hands, leaving them with the feeling of catching a shot put or, as Dilfer put it, "a wet brick."

Passing aficionados say this is a result of Tebow throwing with too much arm action. Because of Tebow's lengthy release, his whole arm needs to come forward with his throw. Quarterbacks such as Manning, who release the ball from near the ear hole of their helmet, also have more butt, legs and hip torque involved in their throws. The more a quarterback gets his body behind the throw, the easier it is to control the aim and velocity.

"The length of his stroke is not nearly as concerning as the actual snap of the ball off his hand," Dilfer said. "The reason why he doesn't always get good spin is he never rolls his wrist right when he takes it back. Keeps his wrist flat. A lot of players see it but they don't know why. The why is they never load properly."

And then there are the more obvious problems with a long delivery. The longer it takes to release the ball, the more vulnerable a quarterback is to getting sacked or getting the ball swatted out of his hand.

"If you can't refine his delivery, then he's going to struggle to become a consistent quarterback anywhere," said Joe Theismann, the former Washington Redskins' Super Bowl champion quarterback and longtime NFL analyst. "I've seen Tim Tebow play, and I've spoken to guys who have worked with him. And they love him to death. What isn't there to love? Big, strong, great work ethic

> "I'm not out there (at Broncos practices). I'm talking from a distance. But I know from experience that **a guy like Tebow definitely makes a difference."**
>
> **Dan Reeves**, former Broncos head coach

EXPERTS WERE DIVIDED ON WHETHER TEBOW WOULD BE ABLE TO CORRECT HIS THROWING FLAWS. *John Leyba, The Denver Post*

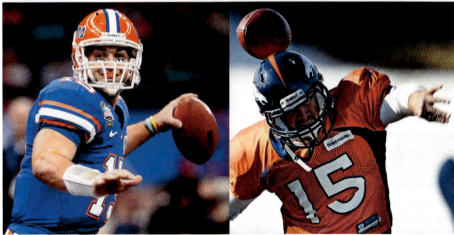

Dave Martin, The Associated Press *John Leyba, The Denver Post*

and the first throw he makes is a great throw. But mechanically, you can't put yourself in the situation where you're susceptible to losing the football."

The exact problem with Tebow's release?

"It's long and low," Theismann said. "Randall Cunningham had a long windup. Tim's is long and low. The ball is away from his body an awful long time. And so it's exposed to danger an awful long time."

Losing the ball because of his long release came into play only once through Tebow's first two seasons. In a 45-10 home drubbing administered by Detroit on Oct. 30, defensive end Cliff Avril swatted the ball out of Tebow's left hand as the quarterback reared back to throw. Avril recovered the fumble and returned it 24 yards for a touchdown.

For all the critique about Tebow's release, though, this is what he told Legwold at the Senior Bowl, when asked about the one aspect of his game he needs to improve: "Probably the footwork. The play-action, just doing all that from under center is different. That's probably been the issue more than the (throwing motion)."

Tebow's footwork remains an ongoing issue, with three main problem areas.

• Like a baseball pitcher who sometimes will "fly open" with his lead shoulder while delivering a pitch, Tebow will sometimes have his feet pointed toward the sideline, say, when he's throwing a pass down the seam. This affects his accuracy. In particular, it's the action of pulling away from center and positioning his

"I've come around

because I strongly discounted his will to improve. In the last two weeks, he's been a totally different player."

Trent Dilfer, after Tebow led Denver past Chicago for a sixth consecutive win

hips and shoulders to throw during the dropback that gives Tebow problems. At Florida, he did not take many snaps under center, instead operating the read-option, spread offense from the shotgun.

As a pro, he's learning footwork, which is about as easy as an infant learning to speak. When passing after taking a five- or seven-step drop, Tebow has developed a tendency to throw with his hips open, resulting in the ball sailing.

This action of flying open also causes Tebow to throw from a dropped release. Instead of throwing over the top, his release is often more of a sidearm delivery, causing the pass to sail.

• Timing. A receiver that is running, say, a seven-step slant will time with a quarterback taking a three-step drop. In his early development stage, Tebow sometimes would not "stick" his footsteps. He tended to drift, which caused him to hurry his delivery when his back foot wasn't set or was planted in a way that he would throw too much off the back foot.

• Former NFL coach Herm Edwards, now an ESPN analyst, once said it looked to him as if Tebow's back foot wasn't tied to his throwing release. Dilfer said proper footwork starts with a quarterback's vision of the field.

"It's all his eyes," Dilfer said. "Your eyes speak to your feet. When you understand what you see and you're looking at the right things, your feet will have a quiet rhythm. A big thing for a quarterback is when you're seeing it right, your feet are right, your back arm releases in rhythm with how you set your feet."

The upshot to all this? Tebow's throwing motion won't be used in any instructional video.

You would, though, want him leading your team on a final drive if it needed a score late to win the game.

Tebow may be a mechanical mess. But Steve Young, whose funky lefty delivery and mobility made him the quarterback Tebow fans hope their guy could one day emulate, had three touchdown passes and eight interceptions in his rookie year with Tampa Bay at age 24. A year later, Young had eight TD passes and 13 interceptions.

Following a trade to San Francisco, where coaching wizard Bill Walsh was enamored with Young's athleticism, the eventual Pro Football Hall of Famer got spot playing time until becoming a full-time starter at age 30.

Tebow was 24 this past season when he guided the Broncos to an 8-5 record as a starter, a winning record that included six fourth-quarterback comebacks and a dramatic overtime win over Pittsburgh in the playoffs.

The people who thought they knew what it took to play quarterback in the NFL? They were suddenly learning through Tebow that there is more than one way to succeed. An unconventional way.

"I've come around because I strongly discounted his will to improve," Dilfer said after Tebow led the Broncos to their sixth consecutive victory, against Chicago. "In the last two weeks, he's been a totally different player."

Which is why the caustic analysis was so difficult to comprehend in the first place. Sure, Tebow looked rough throwing the ball during his rookie year and most of his second season. He still does. But analysts were using terms like "never" and "no way."

Was Tebow not allowed to struggle early and improve like everyone else? Elway, after all, threw seven touchdown passes and 14 interceptions as a rookie. Tebow, through his first two seasons, including 16 starts, had 19 TD passes and nine interceptions. Tebow's combined passing and rushing totals for 2011 in 13 starts: 2,788 yards and 19 touchdowns.

"The conflict this offense puts on defenses, he'll never have to be the most accurate passer to be successful," Dilfer said.

"Now, please understand the difference between a scrambler and designed runner. Totally different beats. A scrambler is just improvisation. Trying to make something happen. A designed runner dictates what the defense will do. When you're established as a designed runner, there is more space in the defense. Period. You never have to be as accurate as everybody else."

You just have to win. And the Broncos were about to give Tebow the chance he'd waited his whole life to get.

AFTER ANOTHER MIRACLE COMEBACK LATE IN THE CHICAGO GAME, TEBOW WAS CHANGING EXPERTS' OPINIONS. *John Leyba, The Denver Post*

IT WAS ELWAY WHO SUGGESTED THE CLOCK IS TICKING TOWARD TEBOW TIME

Elway and Fox sat down for a talk. The topic: Tim Tebow. It wasn't a formal, roll-up-the-sleeves, time-to-address-the-elephant-in-the-room talk.

But you'd be surprised how many decisions are made during informal chats.

It was Monday, Sept. 26, the day after the Broncos lost 17-14 at Tennessee, in large part because they failed to score after having first-and-goal at the 2 early in the fourth quarter.

Orton's stat line looked good, 24-of-39 passes with touchdowns thrown to Matt Willis and Willis McGahee. But he also killed one drive with an interception, and on the Broncos' final possession, with a chance to tie or win the game, Orton had a pass tipped that was intercepted, securing defeat. It may not have been Orton's fault the ball got deflected. But with some players, it's always something.

The loss at Tennessee left the Broncos 1-2. Up next were the juggernaut Green Bay Packers, the defending Super Bowl champions, at Lambeau Field. Green Bay was steamrolling teams on its way to a 3-0 start.

Realistically, the Broncos were staring at 1-3.

And so Elway gave Fox a little nudge: Better start getting Tebow a look in practice.

"I said if this thing keeps going the way it's going, we're going to have to make a change," Elway recalled.

And to think fans hammered Elway all season for not showing Tebow enough support. It was Elway who gave him his first shove.

TIM TEBOW WAS ABOUT TO GET MORE REPS IN PRACTICE. IT WAS HIS TIME. *John Leyba, Denver Post*

BRIAN XANDERS, JOHN ELWAY AND MIKE BLUEM WATCHED FROM ON HIGH. ELWAY SENSED SOMETHING WRONG WITH KYLE ORTON'S LEADERSHIP. HE URGED COACH JOHN FOX TO GET TIM TEBOW READY – JUST IN CASE. *John Leyba, The Denver Post*

The Packers destroyed the Broncos 49-23, although Orton did play well early. He threw two touchdown passes to Eric Decker in the second quarter to get the Broncos within 21-17. There was a third touchdown pass to tight end Daniel Fells. In all, Orton was 22-of-32 for 273 yards and three TDs. But he also threw three interceptions, including one that Packers star cornerback Charles Woodson returned 30 yards for a touchdown.

It wasn't easy to quantify, or describe, but something just didn't seem right within the team. More and more, Orton was getting that dreaded label of "playing just well enough to lose." Already, this early in the season, the team, at 1-3, seemed resigned to defeat.

Maybe it was the slow start combined with going 4-12 in 2010 and going 2-8 in the final 10 games of the previous season. Dating to Nov. 1, 2009, the Broncos were an abysmal 7-23.

No wonder some players felt beaten down.

Plus, Orton seemed to be gradually losing confidence, especially when the team needed him most. In the season opener against Oakland, the ball dropped out of his hands as he cocked to throw to a wide-open Fells in the fourth quarter. Execute that play and the Broncos probably win. Instead, the Raiders recovered the unforced fumble and won 23-20.

In Game 3 at Tennessee, the Broncos led 14-10 and had first-and-goal at the Titans' 2-yard line early in the fourth quarter. On first down, Orton threw the ball away when his first option was covered instead of scanning the field for another receiver. Willis McGahee then carried three times while Tebow, arguably the best short-yardage weapon in football, watched from the sideline. The Titans held and later took the lead. Orton, as was his habit going back to the 2010 season opener at Jacksonville, failed to move the Broncos on their final drive.

Wrote Mike Klis in The Denver Post's game account:

Afterward, the Broncos' locker room was the quietest it's been in years. It's never exactly reverberating with boom-box music after any defeat. But based on the utter silence in the locker room a good 25 minutes after the final gun Sunday, this setback was more difficult than others.

• • •

No one really blamed Orton. After all, it wasn't his fault McGahee and the offensive line couldn't punch it in near the goal line. But, for all the coachspeak that football is a team game, here's the truth about the NFL: The quarterback is responsible for winning games.

The rest of the players block and tackle and sweat and toil. They do all the dirty work, but in the end, they need their quarterback to reward all that effort.

Orton was not often enough rewarding his team. Elway, whose fourth-quarter comebacks became the identity of his career, sensed this flaw in Orton's game.

And so he got together with the man he hired, Fox, to discuss what-if scenarios.

Elway was more aware of the growing Tebow chatter outside the building than Fox. To some extent, a man in Elway's position must detach himself from the day-to-day grind. Yes, he watches the team's practices every day. But top executives are supposed to watch from on high. He'll have a suggestion here and there and pass it on to Fox. But as a former player, he appreciates bosses who don't micromanage.

Besides, Elway's job is to not only make decisions that are best for the franchise in the short term, but are best for the franchise years out. What's best for this year and what's best for the long term often are in conflict.

Playing Tebow, for instance.

Fox, like all NFL coaches, spends his entire workweek preparing for

THE DRUBBING AT LAMBEAU LEFT THE BRONCOS 1-3 ON THE SEASON. TEBOW WOULD SOON ASSUME CONTROL. *Joe Amon, The Denver Post*

game day. He's not thinking about who his quarterback will be in 2012. His complete focus, during Packers week, was getting Orton prepared to face the champions.

The subject of Elway's talk to Fox – playing Tebow – immediately became evident. At his weekly Monday news conference, Fox said he would start using a specific Tebow "package." At the time, people thought Fox's reconsideration of playing Tebow, at least on a part-time basis, was a reaction to the Broncos' four-down, goal-line failure at Tennessee. It was, but what was unknown at the time is that it also was a result of the talk Fox had with Elway that playing Tebow on a full-time basis might not be too far off.

Against the Packers, Tebow got only one designed rushing attempt, for minus-1 yard, before Fox abandoned the Tebow package. But little did anyone know that the Tebow seed had already been planted.

After the butt-whipping in Green Bay, the Broncos headed into a Week 5 home game against rival San Diego, the near-unanimous choice to win the AFC West. Following that game, the Broncos would have their bye week, which would give Denver two weeks to prepare for its next game, Oct. 23 in Miami.

In case, you know, the Broncos thought about giving a certain player two weeks to prepare.

But whether Fox was aware or not, he already was under fire. Denver Post columnist Mark Kiszla was not going to give him the free pass that a new coach usually receives. Because Fox had finished 2-14 in 2010 with the Carolina Panthers, Kiszla believed he should not get the benefit-of-the-doubt excuse of inheriting a team with problems.

THE DENVER POST 53

Wrote Kiszla following the Packers' demolition of the Broncos:

GREEN BAY, WIS. » If the Broncos knew they were doomed to wear this ugly 1-3 record, they could have kept Josh McDaniels in charge, twirling his whistle.

Is John Fox really an improvement over the most-despised coach in franchise history?

You couldn't tell it from this dogday afternoon, when Denver was used and abused as the chew toy of Green Bay quarterback Aaron Rodgers in a lopsided 49-23 loss to the reigning NFL champion.

"That's embarrassing," Denver defensive end Elvis Dumervil said Sunday.

The hoodie is gone. The Broncos still stink.

In his final 20 games before being dismissed as Denver's coach, McDaniels managed a record of 5-15. No wonder the hoodie got canned.

During the most recent 20 games Fox has worked on an NFL sideline, his record is 3-17. In this league, there can be a million ways to rationalize failure, but you ultimately are what your record says you are.

Even the fine folks of Titletown USA decided Fox could use some coaching advice, as scattered chants of "Tee-bow!" were heard at Lambeau Field during the fourth quarter. When Cheeseheads begin telling a visiting coach the lone reason to watch his team, it's probably a sign this Denver season is on the verge of fading to black.

The package the Broncos installed for Tim Tebow amounted to nothing more than a single rush from the shotgun formation in the opening half. The result was a net loss of 1 yard.

"It didn't prove to be very efficient, so we went in a different direction," Fox said.

• • •

The quarterback conundrum, perhaps more than any issue that strikes a professional football franchise, must be handled with sensitivity. The first hope for Elway and Fox was to beat the Chargers. Win, and the Broncos would be 2-3. With winless Miami on the other side of the bye, the Broncos could be back in business at 3-3.

This was plan A.

What happens if the Broncos lose to the Chargers? At that point, the team is 1-4, with the season on the brink, a bye week coming up and all signs pointing to Tebow getting a chance.

No, not because the fans were demanding it, but because the team had invested a first-round draft pick in Tebow a year earlier.

After the 2005 season, San Diego kicked Pro Bowl quarterback Drew Brees to the curb because it had invested a first-round draft pick in Philip Rivers a year earlier. Rivers hardly played in 2004 and 2005. It was time for the Chargers to see what he could do. Similarly, in 2004 the New York Giants quickly gave up on Kurt Warner because they selected Eli Manning with the No. 1 overall draft pick.

Once Brett Favre announced his retirement following the 2007 season, Green Bay general manager Ted Thompson and coach Mike McCarthy slammed the door shut so tight and so quickly that Favre had no chance of getting back on the field with the Packers after changing his mind. Why? Because Thompson and McCarthy had to find out what they had in Aaron Rodgers, a first-round draft pick who sat watching for three years.

Playing first-round draft picks, regardless of whether they're better than the incumbent veteran, is what NFL franchises do. They do it because they have to find out what they have.

The Broncos needed to do the same.

Nothing definitive was set when Elway and Fox finished their talk. But it was understood, if not outright stated, that Orton had better come through sooner rather than later.

If Plan B was Tebow, though, Fox wasn't about to tell the public. Wrote Denver Post reporter Lindsay H. Jones from the loss in Green Bay:

GREEN BAY, WIS. » John Fox said coaches did not consider playing backup Tim Tebow in the fourth quarter, when the Packers led by at least 25 points. The team played several backups on defense late in the game, but none on offense.

"We need our starting quarterback to get experience for us to improve. That's the idea behind that. You know he needs to get better in our system," Fox said. "I know he gets

> "We need our starting quarterback to get experience for us to improve."
>
> **John Fox,** on why he stayed with Kyle Orton in a blowout loss to Green Bay

FANS MADE THEIR FEELINGS KNOWN WHEN THE BRONCOS TRAILED SAN DIEGO 23-10 AT HALFTIME. AAron Ontiveroz, The Denver Post

WILL TO WIN: CHAPTER 5

ORTON HAD DECENT NUMBERS, BUT FEW WINS. *John Leyba, The Denver Post*

judged on the past couple of years, but we're trying to get him better in our system and use that experience to get better."

Orton continued to have the backing of his offensive teammates, who remain hopeful there will be more smooth quarters like the second and fewer mistakes all around, not just by Orton.

"You can't blame it all on the quarterback. We know all his balls aren't going to be perfect, and every decision he's going to make isn't going to be the right decision, but Kyle is our guy," running back Willis McGahee said. "That's who we are going to stick with, regardless of the situation. I have faith in him. I know the whole offense and defense has faith in him."

Orton's three interceptions against the Packers brought his season total to six, with half coming in fourth quarters. He also lost a fumble in the fourth quarter of the season opener.

• • •

The fourth quarter. The Broncos' quarterback performance in the fourth quarter was about to do a 180. And it was about to change a tad sooner than most thought.

In front of their disgruntled home fans Oct. 9, the Broncos were getting whipped 23-10 at halftime by Philip Rivers and the Chargers. Orton played as if he was finished. He had held up pretty well to Tebowmania through the first 16 months, but it appeared he had reached his breaking point.

At the half, he was 6-of-13 for a sorry 34 yards. He had thrown another interception. The Broncos' only touchdown was Cassius Vaughn's 55-yard interception return of an errant Rivers' pass.

The Chargers held the ball nearly 20 minutes. The Broncos needed a jolt. They needed a change.

If it was Elway who nudged Fox,

it was Fox who ultimately made the call. Fox's gut told him it was time. Not after the bye week. Now.

As Broncos players ran into the locker room with boos raining down from their hometown fans, offensive coordinator Mike McCoy ran up alongside Tebow and said, "Get ready. You're up."

Those four words changed the Broncos' season.

Tebow started slowly in the third quarter. The Chargers received the second-half kickoff and, though their first possession ended in a punt, they ate 6:06 off the clock. Tebow had two possessions in the third quarter. Two three-and-outs. He passed three times, completing one, for no yards.

The Chargers' Nick Novak kicked a long field goal early in the fourth quarter, stretching the lead to 26-10. On the Broncos' first possession of the fourth quarter, Tebow threw two more incompletions and the Broncos punted again. By the time the Broncos got the ball near midfield for Tebow's fourth possession, he was 1-of-5 for zero yards. His team was down 16.

Tebow Time. Here's how The Denver Post's Mike Klis wrapped up his game story:

Initially, Tebow missed some passes he should have hit. And then he showed there is more to playing quarterback than passing. Down 26-10 with 8:54 remaining and the ball near midfield, running back Willis McGahee got 28 of his 125 yards – his third 100-yard rushing performance in four games – on the first play.

Tebow took it from there, rushing for 11 yards to the Chargers' 12-yard line, then scrambling into the end zone on the next play. McGahee ran in the two-point conversion, and even though Tebow still had zero yards passing, the Broncos had closed the deficit to 26-18.

After Broncos defensive end Robert Ayers stripped Rivers, Tebow huddled up with the ball at the San Diego 41 and 4:38 remaining.

Again, Tebow and McGahee ran well on successive plays. Next, the southpaw flipped a screen pass to Knowshon Moreno, who charged ahead for a 28-yard touchdown reception.

It was 26-24 with 3:19 remaining. But on the two-point conversion, Tebow's well-thrown fade pattern to Brandon Lloyd was stripped out of the receiver's hands and fell incomplete.

Rivers managed to take nearly three minutes off the clock while moving the Chargers to a game-clinching field goal. The three points became crucial because even though Tebow had just 24 seconds remaining and 80 yards to go, he made two long completions to the Chargers' 30.

With five seconds remaining, Tebow scrambled off the remaining time and several seconds more before his throw into a crowded end zone was knocked down incomplete.

The Broncos had lost. Fans streamed to the exits chanting, "Tebow! Tebow!"

• • •

Never has a loss felt so good.
In the postgame locker room, the feelings were mixed.

Said Von Miller, a rookie linebacker: "I love seeing Tim out there. Everybody watches Tim no matter what he's doing."

But, said Broncos left guard Zane Beadles, speaking on behalf of the offensive line: "Kyle's our guy. And, he's a good friend. Going through something like that is hard. But we have a job to do. And our job is to protect the quarterback. Whoever they put back there at quarterback, we're going to protect him."

Beadles broke in with Orton in 2010. Miller was still at Texas A&M that year. Miller was not as invested in Orton as some of the other Broncos who had been around awhile. Miller was new blood. Tebow was new blood.

A Denver Post sidebar on Orton following the game said:

For all his nonchalance and gritty character, Kyle Orton is human.

And the human condition can take only so much.

As time went on, it appeared the "Tebow Thing" started suffocating Orton's ability to play quarterback.

"I'm a PE major, so I really don't know about all that," Fox said. "You'd have to ask Kyle."

Orton was asked. The Broncos had just lost an AFC West Division game

> **"We know what he's about.**
> With a guy like that, make him beat us with the pass. If he proves he can do that, then good for him, but until he proves that, you play the run."
>
> Chargers free safety **Eric Weddle**

> "People's opinions don't matter to me, man. I left that a long time ago."
>
> **Kyle Orton,** after being replaced by Tebow in the San Diego game

to San Diego 29-24, and Orton had just stood before the cameras, microphones, recorders and rapid-fire questions about his day that ended with a second-half demotion.

After completing only 6-of-13 passes for 34 yards and an interception, Orton was replaced as the starting quarterback by the people's choice, Tim Tebow.

Most people have wanted Tebow since the day he became the No. 25 pick in the 2010 draft. Only Orton was in the people's way. After completing his mob interview session, Orton was in the hallway outside the locker room when he was asked if the fans clamoring for Tebow had gotten to him.

"People's opinions don't matter to me, man," Orton said defiantly. "I left that a long time ago. I've been through that before. I'm just frustrated with the way we were playing, myself included."

Fox did not make it official during his postgame news conference that Tebow would be the Broncos' starting quarterback from this point on. But he likely will make it official Tuesday.

This wasn't bowing to public pressure. This was Fox sticking with Orton until Orton lost the job.

"This is a high-pressure job as a player and as a coach, and we're in a performance-based business and we have to perform," Fox said.

Orton is a free agent after this season. Barring injury, he may well have started his last game for the Broncos.

• • •

Indeed, Orton had taken his last snap for the Broncos.

The Chargers? Bolstered by a victory that improved their record to 4-1, they were defiant. Yes, they struggled to stop Tebow in the fourth quarter, but just wait. They promised his act wouldn't play so well the next time the teams met in San Diego.

Wrote Denver Post columnist Dave Krieger:

Sunday's loss, the Broncos' fourth in five games, was like a lab experiment designed to demonstrate the difference between the way fans view Tebow and the way football professionals view him.

The Chargers also pointed out they would design a different defensive plan for Tebow than the one they brought to Denver for Orton if they knew he would play.

"Believe me, there is a specific game plan you need when you're playing a quarterback like him, and you're torn a little bit when you're facing two," San Diego coach Norv Turner said.

If Tebow is now the Broncos' starter – and given how they've played under Orton, he might as well be – opponents almost certainly will pack the box to stop the run until he proves he can beat them with the pass. Although Tebow had some nice throws Sunday, he also missed several open receivers with throws at their feet.

"We know what he's about," Chargers free safety Eric Weddle said. "With a guy like that, make him beat us with the pass. If he proves he can do that, then good for him, but until he proves that, you play the run. But when you have a lead, you can't give up big plays. You can't stack the box, no help deep, and then you give up an easy touchdown. That's just bad football."

For fans, Tebow is almost a drug. He seemed to make many of them forget that the Broncos are now 1-4, three games out of first place just five games into the season. He provided excitement and hope. He's sort of the Broncos' version of that hopey-changey thing.

The offense under Orton is now in a persistent vegetative state, so there is no reason not to let Tebow continue. But how he fares against defensive game plans designed for his skill set remains an open question.

"It's what I've seen happen in college football," Turner said. "I mean, when two good teams play against each other that are spread teams, the scores go way down. All you've got to do is look at the national championship game; you look at some of these teams that see each other. So familiarity takes care of that, and the more you see it, the more you practice against it, the more you're able to handle it.

"I'm not going to make predictions or speak for anyone, but we play these guys again, and I have a feeling we'll be getting ready for it."

• • •

For an NFL coach, Turner's words were strong. And seven weeks later, when the Broncos and Chargers played again, this time in San Diego, Turner would have to eat those words. Again, it would take an exhilarating finish to prove Turner wrong.

But Turner would be wrong.

THE CHARGERS SAID THEY HAD TEBOW FIGURED OUT AND LOOKED FORWARD TO THE GAME IN SAN DIEGO. *John Leyba, The Denver Post*

YES, TEBOW WAS UNCONVENTIONAL. BUT, HE BEGINS WINNING OVER TEAM

Tebow Time. Most people associate that term with the do-or-die portion of the game when defeat is near, but have no fear – Tim Tebow is here.

Before Tebow Time could start ticking, though, he had to first win over his bosses upstairs. Never mind his teammates in the locker room. Tebow's teammates would buy in as soon as they knew John Elway and John Fox were sold.

There would be some hiccups, even as the Broncos won three of Tebow's first four starts, beating Miami, Oakland and Kansas City, all on the road.

In the victory over the Chiefs, the Broncos raised eyebrows across the NFL by running the ball 55 times and attempting just eight passes. Tebow completed just 2-of-8 passes, a line that would have brought a smile to the late Woody Hayes. One of Tebow's two completions went for a long touchdown to Eric Decker late in the game that clinched a 17-10 victory at Arrowhead Stadium.

The football public was fascinated with the college-style, read-option offense John Fox implemented for what pundits said was a college-type quarterback.

One of those wisecracks came from Fox himself. In the week after the victory over the Chiefs, Fox invited an NFL Network reporter, Jeff Darlington, into his office to watch game tape. The subject got around to the team's new offense. Immersed in the film, an unguarded Fox told Darlington that if the Broncos used a conventional offense, "(Tebow) would be screwed."

Oops. Fox's quote went viral, carrying the sports news for two days leading up to his team's Nov. 17 Thursday night game against the New York Jets.

BRONCOS FANS HAD REASON TO CELEBRATE A WIN IN KANSAS CITY AND THEIR NEW STARTING QUARTERBACK. *John Leyba, Denver Post*

| WILL TO WIN: CHAPTER 6

DESPITE THE BELIEF OF THE BRONCOS' HIERARCHY EARLY IN THE SEASON THAT ORTON GAVE THE TEAM ITS BEST CHANCE TO WIN, ELWAY WAIVED THE VETERAN ON NOV. 22.
John Leyba, The Denver Post

Fox later said he "screwed up" in saying Tebow "would be screwed." Luckily for Fox, his story lost legs when his boss, John Elway, came to the rescue.

The Broncos defeated the Jets 17-13, thanks again to some final-minute Tebow magic. With the Broncos trailing late, Tebow marched the offense 95 yards in 12 plays to the winning score, capping the drive with an exhilarating 20-yard touchdown scramble with 58 seconds left.

Four days later, on his regular Monday morning radio show with Vic Lombardi and Gary Miller on 102.3 FM, Elway was asked if he had a better feeling about knowing who the team's quarterback of the future would be than he did five weeks earlier.

The Broncos were 1-4 five weeks earlier, and 4-1 in the five games since Tebow took over.

"Um, no," Elway said bluntly.

That wasn't the answer many Broncos fans or Tebowmaniacs were hoping for. Fox was off the hook. Now it was Elway's turn to become the target of salvos from Tebow Nation.

**Headline to a Lindsay H. Jones story in the Denver Post:
Jury still out on Tebow
Elway remains unconvinced that the Broncos QB with a 4-1 mark this year is the franchise's future.**

• • •

Elway went on to explain in his radio interview that while he sees Tebow making progress, the quarterback needs to start throwing better on third down. Tebow had completed a woeful 6-of-43 passes on third down, or 14 percent, to that point. Against the Jets, the Broncos were 3-for-13 on third down.

"We can't go 3-for-13 and win a championship," Elway said.

So, what was wrong with that statement? Sounds like something a boss who demands better would say. In this case, though, Elway let a cold, hard fact get in the way of the warmhearted Tebow story. The blogosphere attacked Elway's honesty.

The sense around Denver – and around the country, for that matter – was that Elway and Fox had not "bought in" to Tebow, despite the team's success. And if Elway and Fox had not bought in, how could the guys in the locker room completely sell out for their new quarterback?

While the media kept pushing Fox and Elway to commit to Tebow as the starter beyond 2011, the bosses had no intention of making any long-term decision in the heat of the season, for several reasons.

One, the Broncos were suddenly in the hunt for the AFC West title. Why rush to decisions about the following year?

Two, things change quickly in the NFL. Fox and Elway have been around football long enough to know one play, one injury, can alter a season and completely rewrite a script.

Three, the truth was, Tebow simply didn't have a sufficient body of work to justify a long-term commitment. And the playing experience he had wasn't easy to evaluate. He was terrible at times passing the ball and often ineffective running the offense for 3 to 3½ quarters. To Tebow's credit, he showed a remarkable tenacity, will and improvisational skill to win games late. And, somehow, he found his accuracy as a passer late in games.

To be sure, Tebow was the ultimate gamer. He played his best when the spotlight was the brightest, no doubt. But he was a work in progress.

In three of Tebow's first eight starts, the offense did not score in the first half. In two other games, it had just three points at halftime. That's six first-half points, total, by the offense in five of Tebow's first

TEBOW'S NUMBERS WERE NOT GOOD, BUT IN KANSAS CITY, HE FOUND A WAY TO WIN. *John Leyba, The Denver Post*

eight starts.

And yet, the team was 7-1 in those eight games.

That was another reason why Elway and Fox danced around the 2012 guarantee: He was winning without a vote of confidence. Maybe, Tebow's "I'll show them" spirit was part of his success. Why mess with what's working?

The Broncos bosses' slips of the tongue may have been unfortunate from a PR standpoint, and indeed,

they sent Patrick Smyth, the team's media relations director, into action. Smyth would sit down with Fox and Elway and talk about what was said, why the media fanned the words, and what might be better said in the future regarding the hot-button issue in Denver. Subsequent stories would surface stating how much Fox and Elway supported Tebow. But for substantive proof of support, all anyone needed to do was look at their actions.

On Tuesday, Nov. 22, five days after the victory over the Jets, the team waived Orton.

The Broncos made the move even though they risked Orton winding up with Chicago, whom the Broncos would play on Dec. 11, or Kansas City, their opponent in the regular-season finale. Both teams had lost their starter to injury – Jay Cutler in Chicago, Matt Cassel in Kansas City. Either game could have huge playoff implications. By letting Orton go,

WILL TO WIN: CHAPTER 6

Fox and Elway were saying they believed Tebow could beat whatever team Orton plays for.

"We would not have made this move unless we felt good about Tim," Fox said.

The Broncos also were happy they saved $2.6 million of Orton's remaining salary that was, in the end, picked up by the Chiefs, who were awarded Orton because their claim spot was higher on the waiver order than the other two teams who tried to nab him, Dallas and Chicago.

Another reason for moving Orton is it eliminated awkwardness from the locker room. Tebow was more free to be himself around his teammates without offending Orton. And, Bronco players loyal to Orton could be themselves around Tebow.

"I didn't feel like it was a weight off my shoulders," Tebow said in his season-ending interview.

For the Broncos, there would be no turning back. The safety net was gone. Tebow was the Broncos' quarterback, at least for the rest of the season.

Fox decided to emphatically stamp the team's belief in Tebow by propping his quarterback with an in-house honor. After the victory over the Jets, the Broncos next played at San Diego. Traditionally, at the team meeting the night before a game, Fox asks one player to make a speech. Fox picked Tebow for the duty/honor on Nov. 26 at the team's hotel.

The next day, Tebow again overcame a slow start, rallying the Broncos from a 10-0 first-half deficit. Late in the fourth quarter, Tebow led the Broncos on a sustained drive that resulted in a short, game-tying field goal by Matt Prater with 1:34 remaining. In overtime, Tebow did it again, helping set up a Prater field goal with 29 seconds left in the extra period in a 16-13 victory.

So, what did Tebow say to the team the night before? At the core of his message was Proverbs 27:17.

From Denver Post columnist Mark Kiszla:

"Iron sharpens iron, so one man sharpens another," Tebow said Sunday as he walked the stadium catacombs after yet another victory you had to see to believe.

The Broncos, however, have 100 percent faith that Tebow can lead them to the playoffs after a dismal 1-4 start to this season.

"I've never seen a human who can will himself to win like that," Denver linebacker Von Miller said.

If a quarterback who would rather run than throw can pull off an invitation to the Super Bowl tournament, then Tebow must not only be considered a legitimate Pro Bowl candidate, but also should be mentioned in the discussion of the NFL's most valuable player.

Mixing football with religion is what makes Tebow a lightning rod for controversy. But from praying for the Chargers to miss a potential game-winning field goal to preaching to teammates from the Bible, Tebow seems certain heaven is on his side.

Fox asked Tebow to address the team the night before this AFC West showdown. The quarterback fell back on what he knew best and inspired the troops by quoting from the Old Testament.

"He said iron sharpens iron, and men sharpen other men. And I think that's totally true," Miller said. "He gave us a great speech. We came out (for the game) fired up. And that was a wrap."

As Tebow picked a path from the tiny visiting locker room to the team bus, his crowded route caused him to dart and look for daylight as much as any of his 22 carries against San Diego did. Without breaking stride, Tebow autographed a football handed from a grown man and exchanged a fist bump with a smiling child wearing a Chargers replica jersey.

Tebow, however, was stopped dead in his tracks when told his speech on game's eve had touched the hearts of teammates. "It was a huge honor," Tebow said of being given the opportunity. "I just tried to share from the heart."

• • •

Tebow Time in 2011 officially started in the second half of Game 5 against San Diego.

Getting on the field is the most essential step to becoming a team leader. Next was getting his teammates to believe in him. In this regard, Tebow Time took time.

It's not like Champ Bailey, Brian Dawkins or D.J. Williams are going to look up to Tebow, a second-year player with not yet 16 games, or a full season, worth of starts. It's not like Mario Haggan, Elvis Dumervil or Chris Kuper – players who have been around for at least six seasons – are going to seek out Tebow for advice.

They respect him. They can like him. They've been around enough of the pratfalls of public scrutiny to not

> ## "I've never seen a human
> who can will himself to win like that."
>
> **Von Miller,** rookie linebacker

IRON SHARPENS IRON, TEBOW TOLD THE TEAM BEFORE THE WIN OVER THE CHARGERS IN SAN DIEGO. *John Leyba, The Denver Post*

envy him.

But as far as owning a locker room? That's reserved for the all-powerful leaders in the NFL, the types who can be counted on one hand.

Tom Brady, Peyton Manning and Drew Brees have absolute authority. Philip Rivers is getting there in San Diego, especially since he played in the 2007 AFC championship game seven days after tearing an ACL. About the only non-quarterback who has franchise-type power is Baltimore linebacker Ray Lewis.

"I feel like this is Champ Bailey's team," Tebow said on Jan. 4, 2012, the Wednesday before the Broncos' first-round playoff game against Pittsburgh. "This is Brian Dawkins' team. This is Kuper's team and the guys who have been here for a while and have led us on this run. I think they're the big reason why we're here and playing in the playoffs."

For quarterbacks who aren't among the elite of the elite, they aren't so much the team leader as they are, well, the quarterback. More important than the fullback or left guard, with all due respect to Spencer Larsen and Zane Beadles. But most quarterbacks such as Tebow defer to the likes of Bailey and Dawkins.

Besides, the simple logistics of an NFL locker room make it almost impossible for one guy to control the room. Tebow and the quarterbacks sit in the front row of the locker room as you come in from the front-lobby side of the building. The back half of the locker room belongs to the defensive players.

Guys like cornerback André Goodman and defensive tackle Brodrick Bunkley, who have lockers at the far end of the locker room nearest the entrance that leads to the cafeteria, simply don't see much of Tebow dur-

THE DENVER POST 65

WIDE RECEIVER BRANDON LLOYD HAD A VESTED INTEREST IN SEEING ORTON SUCCEED. WITH TEBOW CALLING SIGNALS, THE BRONCOS WOULD TURN AWAY FROM A PASSING GAME – AND LLOYD'S STATS WOULD SUFFER. *Andy Cross, The Denver Post*

ing a workday.

A guy can't lead what he doesn't see.

Even for an athlete such as Tebow, who exudes leadership, there were other reasons why he would not easily become the boss of the locker room.

First, going back to Tebow's rookie year, it's difficult for any newcomer to meld into his new surroundings when he walks in as the most-hyped player on the planet. Tebow hadn't taken a snap in the NFL, and yet he had commercial and endorsement opportunities a veteran could only dream of, not to mention constant media attention from national and local outlets. So many other players in the room, proven players, had none of that and would never get it.

It can cause resentment.

Tebow knew this. His way of combating the issue was to outwork everyone. He wasn't interested in necessarily becoming "one of the guys" because he doesn't swear, doesn't drink and doesn't chase women. He has his own friends away from the Broncos, most notably his brothers, who moved in with him. But his first major step to becoming a leader was to set the proper example. In his first training camp, with Josh McDaniels in charge, the Broncos ran a ton of conditioning post-practice sprints. Tebow won all of them. Not most of them. Every single one.

This can be dicey, too. Some veterans looked at him as if he was trying to show them up. The "Quit brown-nosing, Tebow!" look. Kids are supposed to know their place. And a kid's place on a professional sports team is behind the veterans, not winning wind sprints.

This unwritten code of rookie conduct, obviously, was in conflict with Tebow's DNA.

"My hope was that if everyone saw that I was consistent, that they'd just think that's the way I am," Tebow said late this past season, when asked to recall his rookie sprint winning streak. "I just go the hardest I can every time. I think it's silly to not do your best for whatever reason there is."

It's also impossible for any player on the bench to become a leader. Detroit Tigers manager Jim Leyland once said the most important aspect to becoming a good leader was becoming a good player. The better the player, the more likely others will follow. You think a rookie cornerback is going to pay attention to how a special-teams reserve prepares? Or will he pay attention to how Bailey, a 10-time Pro Bowl selection, prepares?

Tebow could not take ownership of the locker room until he played. And if he wasn't playing, the locker room would stand behind the quarterback who was playing, which from the first day of training camp was Kyle Orton.

"There's all kinds of rumors that we might trade Kyle, things like that," Chris Kuper, the senior statesman of the Broncos' offensive line, said during the lockout in early July. "But we like Kyle. He played well last year, and I think he's proved he's a starter in this league."

Training camp did not change opinions in the locker room. As camp opened with Orton on the trading block, the unsettled quarterback situation put the rest of the players in an awkward position.

"I've been spending most of my brainpower in this offseason thinking of how to get Tebow better, to help

TEBOW AND HIS LATE-GAME HEROICS ATTRACTED THE MEDIA SPOTLIGHT. *John Leyba, The Denver Post*

him develop as a quarterback," top receiver Brandon Lloyd said as camp was set to open. "Kyle's going to be awesome wherever he goes."

Lloyd's stance was hollow. He thought one way when it appeared Tebow would be the starter and Orton would be traded. When the proposed Orton trade to Miami fell through, Lloyd couldn't unhitch his wagon from Tebow fast enough.

Further motivating Lloyd to push for the "passing-oriented" quarterback was his own below-market contract. He was entering the final year of a deal and getting paid $1.35 million, though he'd made the Pro Bowl the year before with 1,448 yards receiving, mostly from Orton passes.

To get big dollars as a free agent, Lloyd needed stats. And to get stats, he figured Orton needed to be throwing to him. It didn't take Curly Lambeau-like genius to understand the Broncos would eventually have to find out whether Tebow could be a full-time quarterback before the team moved forward, though.

"It's the Tebow Thing," Lloyd told Sports Illustrated's Jim Trotter early in training camp. "They'll put Kyle on the trading block because they don't want to deal with the Tebow Thing. But it's not going to end until he plays."

Clearly, Tebow did not own the locker room early in camp.

It didn't help that he was throwing some of the ugliest passes teammates had seen since their high school days. More than one veteran whispered, off the record, that they didn't think the kid could play.

The Monday following the Broncos' second preseason game, Fox officially named Orton the starter for the season opener against Oakland.

Reported Lindsay H. Jones in The Denver Post:

"The proof's in the pudding, so to speak," Fox said. "He's played very well. He's got great command of the offense. I think he has the most ex-

> "**All I care about is that locker room.** We like all our quarterbacks, highlight all of them. They're all good players."
>
> **John Fox,** after naming Kyle Orton the starter for the preseason's first game

perience in this offense, and I think that's been evident."

• • •

As he walked into the locker room after Monday's practice, Orton said he didn't have a comment about Fox's decision. That is probably because he wasn't surprised.

"We know on the outside there's a lot of talk. This will probably hush the media conversation a little bit," Decker said. "Internally, I think everybody knew that he would probably be the one who got the ball."

Following the Tuesday practice, Fox addressed the media. And, as usual, the media wasn't ready to move on from yesterday's news. Fox's decision to name Orton the starter was not well received by all. Not only was Tebow not the starter, he had dropped to No. 3, behind both Orton and Brady Quinn, for the upcoming preseason game against Buffalo.

"All I care about is in that locker room," Fox said. "We like all our quarterbacks, highlight all of them. They're all good players."

The locker room. Fox knew the locker room wanted Orton because the players saw him outplay Tebow.

Then there was that anonymous source within the team who was quoted as telling Yahoo.com that "if everything was totally equal and this competition were based only on performance at this camp, Tebow would probably be the fourth-string guy. ... I'm telling you, Adam Weber is flat-out better right now."

No one doubted someone within the organization made that statement. But it showed how clueless even the most knowledgeable football men were about Tebow's game.

NFL practices are about running plays as they're drawn up in the playbook. Tebow is not a follow-the-diagram kind of quarterback. It's when the diagrams go off line that Tebow's incredible improvisational skills are showcased.

Which is why it was so shocking that McDaniels drafted him in the first place. McDaniels coaches a systematic offense. Pass patterns are precise with one or two receivers serving as decoys to set up the primary receiver. Tebow is the quintessential chaos quarterback.

Orton? Now there's a system quarterback. Drop back one, two, three. Read the progression, one, two, three. Step up in the pocket, one, two, three. Throw the ball, one, two, three.

All this is fine, except when a pass rusher gets in the way of one, or two, or three.

After Fox announced Orton was his starter, Tebow was asked about his relationship with the man who beat him out.

"Me and Kyle definitely have a good relationship," Tebow said. "We were actually having fun, just enjoying being out there. He's had a very good preseason."

The relationship between Tebow and Orton seemed more chilly than good. But as professionals, neither wanted to stir up a controversy.

Orton didn't play well in the season opener against Oakland. In fact, it can be argued he cost the Broncos the game. His poor throw leading to an interception near the end of the first half set up Sebastian Janikowski's NFL record-tying 63-yard field goal, giving the Raiders a 16-3 lead.

Then, after Orton rallied the Broncos to within 16-13 early in the fourth quarter, Orton had first-and-10 at the Raiders' 24 when he rolled right with the idea of throwing a misdirection pass to the left. Sure enough, tight end Daniel Fells was open on a wheel route. Orton reared back ... and dropped the ball. Dropped it. The Raiders recovered and left town with a 23-20 victory.

Orton threw for 304 yards. Broncos fans had seen this way too many times before, Orton compiling pretty statistics in an ugly loss. Broncos fans were fed up. They wanted Orton out, or at least wanted to see what one of the great winners in college football history could do. But Fox wasn't using Tebow.

Jesse Oaks, a Broncos fan from Independence, Ky., typed on a Broncos message board that he was seeking donations to raise $10,000 so he could rent out two downtown Denver billboards with a message directed at Fox to "Play Tim Tebow."

Inside the locker room, support for Orton was unwavering. The players had seen how poorly Tebow threw in practice. They had seen how well Orton threw in practice. That was something else the fans no longer wanted to hear.

But players, by their nature, back

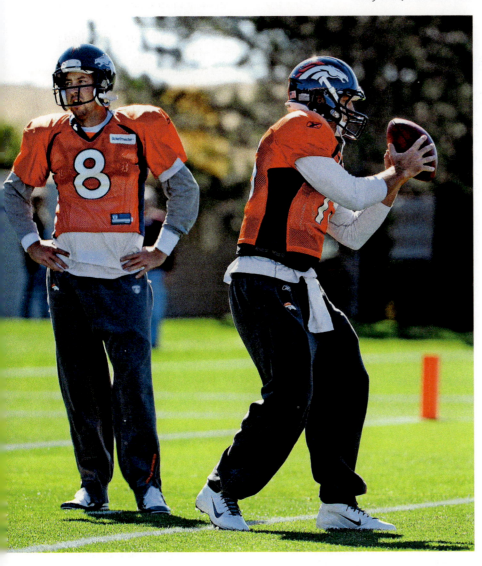

ORTON AND TEBOW HAD A CHILLY BUT PROFESSIONAL RELATIONSHIP.
Andy Cross, The Denver Post

the starting quarterback. It's not personal. It's how players are taught by coaches. Brainwashed even. Orton's teammates, for now, had his back.

Orton rewarded that faith the following week against Cincinnati. Despite injuries forcing the Broncos to play without a who's who list of starters – Champ Bailey, Elvis Dumervil, D.J. Williams, Brandon Lloyd, Knowshon Moreno and Marcus Thomas were out, and then two more starters, Eddie Royal and Julius Thomas, went down early in the game with injuries – the team posted an impressive 24-22 victory.

Tebow? He became the Broncos' No. 3 receiver following the injuries to Lloyd and Royal. He was in for a handful of plays at receiver but never had a ball thrown his way.

"Oh, man, I wanted one so bad," he said.

Fox's faith in Orton fended off the cries for Tebow, for at least another week.

"He keeps his poise and he knows the thing about us is, Orton's our guy," running back Willis McGahee said afterward. "He's going to be our guy from here on out."

As it turned out, "here on out" lasted two weeks.

Still short-handed the next week at Tennessee, the Broncos played well, particularly on defense. They had the lead most of the game. They could have all but clinched victory early in the fourth quarter when they had first-and-goal at the 2, with a chance to take a two-score lead.

One incomplete pass and three McGahee runs left the ball at the 1. No points. Not Orton's fault. He threw a pick on a deflected pass on his final drive, ending the Broncos' final chance in the 17-14 loss.

Not his fault. Over and over again the fans heard how another defeat was not Orton's fault.

This time, the fans went a step further. The billboard went up. The Kentucky fan never did raise enough money, but his idea floated to Mohammad Suleiman of OneSwoosh.com, who along the Interstate 25 northern corridor of Denver put up a digital billboard message that read: BRONCOS FANS TO JOHN FOX: PLAY TEBOW!!
And, FOX: WELCOME TO TEBOW-LAND.

Fox was asked on the Monday after the Tennessee loss if he would stick with Orton.

"As I mentioned earlier, not one guy has got us to where we are," Fox said. "Right now, Kyle, in our opinion, gives us the best chance."

Fox had been saying Orton "gives us the best chance to win" since the first week of camp. Yet the losses were piling up. Orton finished 2009 in a 2-7 skid as a starter. He went 3-10 in 2010. And he was 1-2 with Fox, putting him in a 6-19 rut. This is the guy who gives the team its best chance to win?

Fox got the message. From that point on, he stopped saying Orton gave his team its best chance to win. Soon, Fox stopped playing him altogether. The week after the Tennessee game, the Broncos got trounced in

WILL TO WIN: CHAPTER 6

IN TEBOW'S FIRST START, THE BRONCOS TRAILED MIAMI 15-0. THEN, TEBOW CAUGHT FIRE. *John Leyba, The Denver Post*

Green Bay 49-23.

Orton threw three interceptions.

Late in that game, with a Packers victory well in hand, fans started chanting: "Te-Bow! Te-Bow!" Fox had briefly taken his headset off and heard the chants.

"I thought they were our fans," Fox said later in a quiet hallway at Broncos headquarters. "But I turned around and, nope, they were Packers fans who wanted Tebow. I thought, well, you don't see this every day."

It wasn't just fans who sensed Orton melted under pressure.

Now his teammates were doubting his ability to win. They knew Orton was a better passer than Tebow. They knew Orton was a better quarterback, at least by how they understood the quarterback position should be played. But they remembered how Tebow rallied the team in his three-game audition at the end of the 2010 season. And they knew Orton wasn't getting it done.

The Broncos were 1-3, and a home game against San Diego was next. Orton played terribly in the first half, completing just 6-of-13 passes for 34 yards with an interception. He led the offense to just three points.

Down 23-10 at the half, Fox made a decision. It was Tebow Time. He didn't call it that.

But it was Tebow's play on the field that slowly, gradually started winning over the locker room. He nearly rallied the Broncos from 16 points down against San Diego. Although his game-ending Hail Mary passes fell incomplete, the losing locker room was not smothered by the typical glum atmosphere. There was excitement about what had taken place.

Yes, Tebow looked awful for a long stretch. But there he was, at game's end, heaving the ball into the end zone with a chance to win.

The arrival of Tebow Time meant the departure of Lloyd. With the potential for riches as a free agent looming, Lloyd let management know, through his agent, that he did not want to be part of the run-oriented offense the Broncos would be ushering in with Tebow Time.

Clearly, Broncos bosses felt Lloyd would not be pulling in the same direction as the rest of the team. The bye week coincided with the NFL trading deadline, and Lloyd, the team's top receiver, was gone, dealt to the St. Louis Rams for what became a fifth-round draft pick.

"I think it's a good situation for both sides," Lloyd told The Denver Post shortly after the trade was completed. "(The Broncos) have an opportunity to take a look at their young guys, see what direction they want to go. And I get to go into a system where they pass the ball more."

After the bye week, the Broncos' next game – and Tebow's first start of the season – was at Miami. With 5:23 remaining, the Broncos were sunk. Not only were they down 15-0, Tebow had been awful, having completed just 4-of-14 passes for 40 yards. He didn't just miss open receivers; he was throwing passes into the Dolphins' water coolers. He took five sacks.

And then, somehow, Tebow caught fire. He led the Broncos to 15 game-tying points in the final three minutes, the first time since 1970 that a team overcame a 15-point deficit with less than three minutes remaining.

When Matt Prater boomed a 52-yard field goal in overtime to win it, Tebow knelt in the "Thinking Man" prayer pose to give thanks. The next day, a bunch of guys went on the Internet and started the "Tebowing" craze.

For a week, the nation was hit by

MATT PRATER NAILED A 52-YARD FIELD GOAL IN OVERTIME TO BEAT THE DOLPHINS. TEBOW AND THE BRONCOS WOULD RUN OFF SEVEN WINS IN EIGHT GAMES TO TAKE THE AFC WEST DIVISION LEAD. *John Leyba, The Denver Post*

Tebowing.

Yes, Tebow was getting even more famous by the minute. But the people most important to Tebow, at least to his professional career, were the men he shared a locker room with. He was going to show his teammates that he would not rest on his laurels. The most important step in leading a locker room? Win.

While there were a lot of rolled eyes about how Tebow played for 57 minutes against Miami, it was clear he had started winning over the defensive side of the locker room first.

"I've always been a believer," Broncos rookie linebacker Von Miller said. "He silenced all his critics."

No, Von. Tebow critics will never be silenced. His unconventional methods will always be panned by purists. Purists don't play defense.

"Tebow's amazing, man," Broncos defensive end Jason Hunter said. "An amazing player. He's a playmaker. He won. We support him."

There you go. The players support Tebow. The next week was a disaster, as the upstart Detroit Lions demolished Tebow and the Broncos 45-10. Fox decided after that loss to tweak his offense to better suit Tebow's skills. Fox and his coaches implemented a spread, read-option offense, catching Oakland by surprise. Yes, the Broncos trailed 24-14 late in the third quarter. Tebow Time. By game's end, the Broncos had rolled up 299 yards rushing in a 38-24 victory. Tebow had 118 yards rushing.

"That's hard to defend," Broncos cornerback Champ Bailey said. "Especially when you have a quarterback who's as explosive as Tebow is. Tebow doesn't get enough credit for his explosiveness. I know he would love to sharpen up his passing, but at the same time he's running the ball extremely well."

Tebow didn't get much chance to

"That's hard to defend ...
I know he would love to sharpen up his passing, but at the same time he's running the ball extremely well."

Champ Bailey, after the Broncos rolled up 299 yards rushing against Oakland

sharpen his passes the next week at Kansas City. In a game more suited to the leather-helmet era, Tebow threw eight passes, completing two. But the Broncs won 17-10.

Bad as the Broncos' passing attack looked, Tebow had yet again found a way.

He was starting to earn his teammates' trust. Their confidence in him jumped another level when he again rallied the team to victory over the Jets in a prime-time Thursday night game.

The Broncos were now 4-1 since he took control. Then came the decision to waive Orton and Tebow's "iron sharpens iron" speech. The team was 5-1 with Tebow after the overtime victory in San Diego.

It was the Minnesota game the next week, though, when Tebow started converting everyone, as well as the remaining doubters in the locker room.

Until the Vikings game, Tebow's fourth-quarter comeback wins had come in low-scoring games – 16-13 in overtime, 17-13, 18-15 in overtime. Yes, the Broncos scored 38 points against Oakland, but Tebow was a pedestrian 10-of-21 for 124 yards passing.

The Vikings game was a shootout. A second-half shootout in which Tebow guided the Broncos to 28 points after intermission. They needed them all as Prater, after a late Minnesota turnover, kicked a short field goal at 0:00 for a 35-32 victory.

Once again – and apologies for the repetition – Tebow was miserable in the first half. He completed four passes for 29 yards. He fumbled late in the half to set up a short Minnesota field goal. The Broncos' offense had just one first down. Minnesota led 15-7, with the only Broncos' score coming on a Mario Haggan interception return.

The second half, though, was pure Tebow Time. He completed 6-of-9 passes for 173 yards, including two touchdown passes to Demaryius Thomas.

Tebow didn't just win a shootout. He won a shootout through the air.

The game account, as written by Mike Klis in The Denver Post:

MINNEAPOLIS » If there's justice, Tim Tebow just clinched whatever it was he was supposed to clinch.

After another sensational late-game performance, Tebow lifted the Broncos to a 35-32 victory Sunday against the Minnesota Vikings.

"I've definitely seen that a couple of times from No. 15," said Vikings receiver Percy Harvin, a former Tebow teammate at the University of Florida whose terrific effort – 175 yards from scrimmage and two touchdowns – was spoiled by Tebow leading the Broncos to 28 second-half points. "When I hear all those ESPN commentators say, 'He can't do this,' I laugh. After the game, I whispered in his ear, 'Let 'em keep hating. Keep 'em hating on you.'"

Having lifted a team back from a 1-4 record when it seemingly was in contention for the future quarterback likes of Matt Barkley, Landry Jones or Robert Griffith III, Tebow and his Broncos are now in control of their own playoff destiny.

By virtue of his 6-1 record as a starter that has moved the Broncos (7-5) from last place in the AFC West to a tie with Oakland on top, Tebow has become not just the man of the hour or the Broncos' quarterback of the year.

Has he clinched the right to become their indisputable quarterback of the future?

"Most definitely he should be," said Broncos defensive tackle Marcus Thomas, who also was Tebow's teammate at Florida. "You know I've always been a Tebow man. He's always been going through this where people didn't believe in him. I was criticizing him his freshman year in college."

Wait a minute. Tebow was getting knocked by his fellow Gators?

"Everybody was," Thomas said. "But he always proved us wrong. It was the way he threw. We had Chris Leak, and Tebow would come in throwing the way he throws. We'd be like, 'Oh, man, he can't do this.' But everything about him is a winner. Ever since his freshman year, we all knew he was the real deal. He proved us all wrong."

• • •

Tim Tebow was proving to be an acquired taste. An exotic, strange taste. For a two-month stretch, everyone inside the Broncos' locker room was drinking the Tebow Kool-Aid.

But by season's end, as the Broncos limped into the playoffs with a three-game losing streak, there was reason to wonder if Elway and Fox wouldn't soon be shopping for an alternative.

ANOTHER GAME, ANOTHER TWO-POINT CONVERSION, ANOTHER WIN, THIS ONE IN MINNEAPOLIS. *John Leyba, The Denver Post*

FAITH IS TEBOW'S ROCK. BUT SOME CAN'T RESIST CASTING STONES

Tebow doesn't just work out. He works out until he is the best-conditioned athlete in football.

During practice, he doesn't lightly jog from station-to-station between periods. He sprints. He works out after the team's workout. On the players' day off on Tuesdays, Tebow works out with his performance coach, Loren Landow.

And Tebow doesn't just play football. He plays for victory and will compete until the last second, until victory is his or until the clock runs out.

So it shouldn't surprise anyone that as a Christian, Tebow strives each day to be the best Christian he can be. As scripture says in the Book of Matthew, one of the Bible's four Gospels, it is not necessarily enough to be a good guy who helps others. It is a Christian obligation to spread the word. To disciple. To perform missionary work. To evangelize.

"After every game, I thank my Lord and savior, Jesus Christ, then I thank my coaches and then teammates," Tebow said in front of his locker during a discussion about his faith. "I'm nothing without them. I do that in case maybe just one person comes to the Lord. I don't try to be offensive about it."

After Tebow rallied the Broncos to a late comeback victory over Chicago, the first question he got at his postgame news conference was his thoughts about what just happened.

"I guess, first and foremost, I'd like to thank my Lord and savior, Jesus Christ, and after that I just want to thank my teammates and coaches," Tebow said.

TEBOW NEVER HESITATES TO GIVE CREDIT AND THANKS TO HIS LORD. *John Leyba, The Denver Post*

WILL TO WIN: CHAPTER 7

NOT EVERYONE APPRECIATES HOW TEBOW EXPRESSES HIS FAITH. JAKE PLUMMER, WHO EXHIBITED HIS OWN BRAND OF INDEPENDENCE, TOLD A RADIO STATION AUDIENCE THAT TEBOW COULD COOL IT A BIT WITH HIS EVANGELIZING. *Denver Post file photo*

> "... when he accepts the fact that **we know that he loves Jesus Christ,** then I think I'll like him a little better."
>
> **Jake Plummer,**
> former Broncos quarterback

After he had played the worst game of his career, throwing three interceptions and losing a fumble (two of the mistakes were returned for touchdowns) in an embarrassing 40-14 loss on Christmas Eve at Buffalo, Tebow was asked what went wrong in the second half.

"Well, first and foremost," he said, "I just want to thank my Lord and savior, Jesus Christ. Isn't it great that no matter what, win or lose, we can still have a chance to celebrate my savior's birth tomorrow? That's very cool. That's something I'm really excited about, celebrating Christmas. That's going to be a lot of fun. As far as to answer your question ... "

Not everyone likes the way Tebow expresses his faith. For some, it's too much. Not all Catholics and Protestants agree with Tebow evangelizing, even if it's normally a short sound bite.

Former Broncos quarterback Jake Plummer was asked about Tebow by a Phoenix radio sports station (XTRA 910) on Nov. 22 – the same day the Broncos waived Orton, by the way. Plummer praised Tebow as a winner, but as Plummer continued to talk, he went there. He went to Tebow's faith.

"Tebow, regardless of whether I wish he'd just shut up after a game and go hug his teammates, I think he's a winner and I respect that about him," Plummer said. "I think that when he accepts the fact that we know that he loves Jesus Christ, then I think I'll like him a little better. I don't hate him because of that. I just would rather not have to hear that every single time he takes a good snap or makes a good handoff."

During his playing days, Plummer was often characterized as a rogue character. He took pride in exhibiting his independence, whether it was growing long hair and a beard while leading the Broncos to the 2005 AFC championship game, arguing with coach Mike Shanahan on the sidelines, or flipping the bird to a home fan in the stands.

Plummer, as much as anyone, preached how a guy can only be himself. Yet, he was criticizing Tebow for being himself.

For some reason, Tebow's strong Christian beliefs have become easy targets for mockery. Even "Tebowing," which began as young men honoring Tebow for the way he honors the Lord, quickly turned into people mocking "Tebowing" – which its creators defined as kneeling in prayer in surroundings that aren't ordinarily places for worship.

When the Detroit Lions' Stephen Tulloch sacked Tebow a few days after the Tebowing craze went viral, he celebrated the sack by dropping into a Tebowing pose. Tebowing in front of Tebow.

Political satirist Bill Maher denigrated Tebow's beliefs. After the

DETROIT'S STEPHEN TULLOCH CELEBRATED A SACK OF TEBOW BY DROPPING INTO A TEBOWING POSE. *AAron Ontiveroz, The Denver Post*

Bills whipped the Broncos, Maher tweeted: "Wow Jesus (expletive) Tim Tebow bad! And on Xmas Eve! Somewhere in hell Satan is Tebowing, saying to Hitler, 'Hey, Buffalo's killing them.'"

Comments such as those don't cause Tebow to change his ways. It hurts, sure. But Tebow answers to no man. He answers to a higher calling.

Besides, statistics say those who assail Tebow for his Christianity are a vocal minority. An estimated 78 to 85 percent of Americans adhere to Christianity. That doesn't mean all American Christians express their faith outwardly. To the contrary, some believe their faith in Jesus as the son of God should be demonstrated humbly, even privately.

The Great Commission in the Book of Matthew, though, pushes Christians to spread the word.

"Tim Tebow does a great job of understanding his role in God's place," said Gus Gill, pastor of Hillside Community Church in Golden. "He's a football player, and he's not just living God's word, he's sharing it. Genuinely. Which is what good

THE DENVER POST 77

> "... he's not just living God's word, he's sharing it. Genuinely. Which is what good evangelism is. **It's who he is.** It's an expression of who he is."
>
> Gus Gill, pastor of Hillside Community Church in Golden

evangelism is. It's who he is. It's an expression of who he is."

To understand how a person ticks, you must become familiar with that person's upbringing. It doesn't take a study in Freud to realize that in most cases, parents are at the root of a person's life. It absolutely is true in the case of Tim Tebow.

His father, Bob, and mother, Pam, met while both were students at the University of Florida. Bob and Pam became Mr. and Mrs. Tebow in the midst of attending a graduate school focusing on ministry. Dad was a pastor at a church in Jacksonville when he took a mission trip to the Philippines, a country of thousands of small islands that is American-friendly going back to before World War II.

Although 80 percent of Filipinos are Roman Catholic, there is a concentrated Muslim base on the island of Mindanao, which is where Bob Tebow set up his family and ministry as a permanent residence in 1985. While there, Bob Tebow not only administered the gospel, he started churches and orphanages. Although the Tebows moved back to Jacksonville in 1990 when Timothy was three, Bob's work continues there today through his Bob Tebow Evangelistic Association.

Tim Tebow made his first missionary trip to the Philippines when he was 15 years old, and he's made several trips since. His foundation is combining with CURE International to build a children's hospital and surgical facility in the Philippines, with construction scheduled to begin in January 2012 and completed in the summer of 2013.

In his NFL column published in the Sunday, Dec. 4 editions of The Denver Post, Mike Klis addressed Tebow's spiritual beliefs by calling on Bill McCartney, whose unprecedented success as coach of the Colorado Buffaloes was often tinged with controversy because of how his outspoken Christian convictions clashed with those at a liberal-minded university.

Wrote Klis:

In this state of mountains, snow, sunshine and so much beauty that so many call it God's country, there are two men who are known as much for their unwavering faith as their prodigious accomplishments in football.

One is Bill McCartney. The other is Tim Tebow.

Like everyone else, McCartney, the long-retired University of Colorado head coach, watches Tebow. McCartney observes closely, only in his case, with a coach's eye. The Broncos have gone from 1-4 when Tebow wasn't the starting quarterback to 5-1 with Tebow in charge.

"I believe one man with his heart on fire can set others on fire," McCartney said. "One man can make a dramatic difference."

While covering the Broncos' locker room, I've noticed a concentrated push in recent weeks to credit the team's turnaround to the defense. The sense is that one player is getting too much credit, and so in an effort to keep the other 52 players happy, Fox and others have stressed team.

Understandable. But too bad. If the defense wanted credit, it should have played well before Tebow took control.

Yes, there are many reasons why the Broncos' game in Minnesota today suddenly has enormous playoff implications. And there is only one reason. Tebow.

When McCartney was talking about the contagiousness of one man with a burning heart, he was not referring to Tebow's spiritual beliefs. He was talking about Tebow's competitive spirit that believers and nonbelievers can understand. It's the same competitive ferocity that McCartney saw from his tailback, Eric Bieniemy, early in the 1990 season at Texas. The Buffs were 1-1-1 at the time, losing 19-14 late in the third quarter, and the Longhorns were driving inside the red zone when Bieniemy decided right then to impose his will.

First, he huddled his offense.

"I mean, it was a commotion on our sidelines," McCartney said.

Then as the quarter ended, the Longhorns' offense ran down to the other end, where they were greeted by a roaring crowd readying for the game-clinching touchdown.

The Buffs' defense, meanwhile, was in a collective walk.

"And I saw something I've never seen happen before or since," McCartney said.

The Buffs' offense comes running

TEBOW JOINS WITH OTHERS BEFORE AND AFTER GAMES TO PRAY. *John Leyba, The Denver Post*

out on the field. There are 22 guys huddling on the field. The 5-foot-6 Bieniemy is somewhere in the middle, the only guy talking.

The defense held Texas to a field goal. The Buffs' offense gets the ball and scores in seven plays. The Buffs' defense, for the first time all game, stops the Longhorns on a three-and-out. The Buffs' offense scores again. The Buffs win.

There were countless reasons why the Buffs went on to win the national championship that season. And there was one reason.

"You cannot underestimate the impact we have on each other," McCartney said. "Listen to this now. This is a quote from Tebow, it was in your paper. It came out April 25, 2010. Listen to what he says now: 'I'm going to have one goal, and that goal is to earn the respect from my teammates and my coaches. That's the only goal I have,' Tebow said. 'It's not to be the starting quarterback right now. It's to earn the respect' – now watch this – 'because when you earn the respect from people, then they begin to like you. Then they believe in you. Then they begin to love you. And then you have a team that's united and cares about each other more than anything else.' "

McCartney paused.

"I believe that stuff."

McCartney believes in what Tebow believes. It is their belief in not just God, but Jesus as the son of God, that has sparked some public condemnation.

"It's a dividing line," McCartney said. "You're either all in or not in at all. That's always been a dividing line. What I like about the way he handles himself is he's not ashamed of his faith. Just because you may not agree with his faith does not cause

WILL TO WIN: CHAPTER 7

FANS, PLAYERS AND TALK-SHOW HOSTS HAD FUN WITH TEBOW'S RELIGIOUS BELIEFS – AND SOME JUST SIMPLY RIDICULED HIM. NONE OF IT SEEMED TO AFFECT TEBOW. AS A GOOD CHRISTIAN, IT WAS HIS JOB TO SPREAD THE WORD. *John Leyba, The Denver Post*

fashion.

Down 15-0 with three minutes to go, Tebow not only suddenly got hot, the Broncos recovered an against-the-odds onside kick and went on to beat Miami in overtime. Against San Diego, a fumble by Broncos tight end Daniel Fells was recovered by defensive tackle Tommie Harris, who lost the ball as he took off running, and the ball bounced into the arms of Denver offensive tackle Orlando Franklin, who had been running 20 yards downfield.

Against Chicago, the Broncos were down 10-7 at the two-minute warning with no timeouts remaining and Chicago with the ball. But Bears running back Marion Barber inexplicably ran out of bounds to stop the clock, giving Tebow enough time to move the Broncos into Matt Prater's field-goal range. Prater made a 59-yarder — 59 yarder! — with three seconds remaining to tie it, then won it in overtime with a 51-yard kick.

It was as if there was Te-vine Intervention.

After the latest miracle, against the Bears, Denver Post columnist Mark Kiszla wrote his take:

The magic of Tim Tebow is bigger than football and grows larger with each late-game miracle by the Broncos. Logic fails to explain this no-way-in-heaven, overtime victory against Chicago, unless you consider: Denver played as if victory were preordained.

"I believe in a big God and special things can happen," Tebow said Sunday after the Broncos defeated the Bears 13-10, only because the Broncos believed they couldn't lose.

How deeply do the Broncos believe?

Well, here's a story certain to cause churchgoers to thump a Bible with a loud "Amen!" and skeptics to roll their eyes at the crazy thought of

him to go into a closet. He's genuine, he's wholehearted, he's authentic.

"If he wasn't, the people in that huddle and in that locker room would have him for lunch. Trust me on this one: When you go in that locker room and you're not who you appear to be, they will take you apart. There's a lot of guys on that team who are not believers. But they

see he's genuine, so that doesn't offend them."

The Broncos are 6-5. They had been 1-4. Until Tebow.

• • •

As the comebacks mounted, it wasn't only Tebow's success amid immense critical fire that captivated a nation, but how he won. The Broncos kept winning in, well, miraculous

WESLEY WOODYARD FORCES A FUMBLE. TEBOW HAD TOLD WOODYARD THAT GOD HAD SPOKEN TO HIM. *Joe Amon, The Denver Post*

mixing religion with sports.

"Tebow came to me and said, 'Don't worry about a thing,' because God has spoken to him," linebacker Wesley Woodyard told me in a quiet corner of the Denver locker room.

With his right hand, Woodyard desperately reached out and ripped the football from the grip of Chicago's Marion Barber just as it appeared he was going to bust a big run to put the Bears squarely in scoring position during the opening minutes of overtime.

The fumble luckily fell into the possession of defensive end Elvis Dumervil, and the Broncos promptly marched downfield to a game-winning, 51-yard field goal by Matt Prater that rocked Denver with a soul-shaking thunder not heard since the local baseball team rode Rocktober to a World Series berth in 2007.

"Don't flipping ask me how this is happening," Broncos cornerback Champ Bailey said, "because you know I don't have the answer."

If you ask Woodyard, these strange bounces are more than a curious roll of random good fortune, but rather a thread running through a stretch of eight games during which Denver has won seven times, each victory more preposterous than the last.

On the evening of Nov. 17, as the Broncos prepared to take the field for warm-ups against the New York Jets, Woodyard looked up from his locker and saw Tebow walking directly toward him with a purpose.

"Kinda weird," Woodyard thought at the time, because a quarterback seldom hangs in the end of the room where defenders dress. Tebow, however, wanted to share a secret and the gospel of strength.

"I gave him a big hug and told him thank you," Woodyard said. "God speaks to people to reach other people."

The Broncos saw themselves in the playoffs when nobody else in the NFL could imagine it.

"It's not necessarily prophesying," Tebow said. "But sometimes you can feel God has a big plan."

What if football wasn't unscripted drama but a movie directed from heaven? Got to admit, I don't buy it. But some Broncos do.

"For all the Tebow haters: You better start believing," Woodyard said.

• • •

Some people may read the column and roll their eyes. God spoke to Tebow? God spoke to Tebow who spoke to Woodyard with the message not to worry? God spoke to Tebow who spoke to Woodyard who was not

THE DENVER POST 81

WILL TO WIN: CHAPTER 7

to worry and then stuck his hand out and caused Marion Barber to fumble?

Those who have their own idea about how God works often say something like: Isn't God a little busy to be worrying about a football game? There are true believers, though, who would come back with the fact, according to the Bible, that God is omniscient. He is everywhere.

In the same second, God can accompany flood victims in the Philippines and watch over a fight on the street corner in the Bronx and witness the 49ers taking on the Seahawks at Candlestick Park.

Christians do believe if they pray enough, God will answer. He will reveal himself to them.

But don't misunderstand Tebow's faith as a cure-all. He does not believe everything will go his way just because he prays for it.

"People often seem to think that when you're following the Lord and trying to do his will, your path will always be clear, the decisions smooth and easy, and life will be lived happily ever after and all that," Tebow wrote in his autobiography, "Through My Eyes." "Sometimes that may be true, but I've found that more often, it's not. The muddled decisions still seem muddled, bad things still happen to believers and great things can happen to nonbelievers. When it comes to making our decisions, the key that God is concerned with is that we are trusting and seeking him."

Consider the pressures Tebow confronts every day as a football player. He has the pressure of playing quarterback. He has the pressure of living up to those who say he is great and the pressure of dealing with the hurtful criticism from those who say he can't throw or can't play or can't win. He has the pressure of trailing late in the fourth quarter.

And he handles them all. In fact, in his short NFL career, Tebow may be the most clutch, poised-under-pressure player Denver has seen since Elway retired as a quarterback following the 1998 season.

And Elway wasn't swarmed with nearly the public scrutiny that Tebow endures.

"I've never seen anything like it," Elway said of the enormous publicity, good and bad, that Tebow receives.

Only Tebow doesn't "endure" the heat so much as he thrives on it.

Tebow said he frees himself from pressure because he plays for the man upstairs. Is it possible that Tebow, and not the local convenient store selling lottery tickets, holds the secret?

When he was asked about his poor performance against the Bills on Christmas Eve, Tebow handled the difficult question by surrendering to it.

"Something that my mom taught me a long time ago, give the praise to the Lord and give your disappointments to the Lord," Tebow said. "That's the number one way I can deal with it. Tomorrow, I still get to celebrate my savior's birth. Ultimately, I don't know what the future holds, but I know who holds my future. That is something that gives me a lot of peace and a lot of comfort when there might be a lot of turbulence around me."

There is always turbulence around Tebow.

Tebow lovers and Tebow haters. He doesn't ask for any of it. But he doesn't hide from it, either.

"The reason why I think God trusts Tim with his success is, look at his family," McCartney said. "What they've done is lay down their lives for people in need. He grew up traveling to these poor countries with desperate needs, and he's seen his parents help these people. So that's the core of who he is."

That faith kept him strong as he faced the first big crisis of his career after taking over as the Broncos' quarterback.

> "People often seem to think that when you're following the Lord and trying to do his will, your path will always be clear, the decisions smooth and easy, and life will be lived happily ever after and all that. Sometimes that may be true, but **I've found that more often, it's not.**"
>
> **Tim Tebow,** in his book "Through My Eyes"

TEBOW'S FAITH PREPARES HIM TO HANDLE ADVERSITY. *John Leyba, The Denver Post*

STATS WERE ADDING UP AGAINST THE IDEA OF TEBOW AS SAVIOR; OAKLAND ON DECK

Tebow did not know it, but after just two starts, he was in danger of losing his job. Maybe he did know it. Broncos coach John Fox wasn't exactly talking like he was putting a consolatory arm around his kid quarterback's shoulder after a 45-10 home thumping at the hands of the Detroit Lions on Oct. 30.

As the Denver Post's Lindsay H. Jones reported following Fox's Monday news conference:

Tim Tebow's NFL audition will continue, at least through Sunday's game at Oakland.

"For this week, yes," Broncos coach John Fox said.

• • •

Just this week? Fox was giving Tebow a third start. But the coach also had come up with a tentative plan in which Tebow would not finish what he started.

If Tebow played poorly in the first half against Oakland in the next game – specifically, if Tebow continued struggling on third downs – Fox was going to yank him and put in Brady Quinn. Orton, by this time, had been demoted to third-string. If Tebow twisted an ankle or struggled, Quinn would be the next man up.

It wasn't just the loss to the Lions that had tested Fox's faith in Tebow. It was how inept Tebow had been for the first 55 minutes of his first start, against the Dolphins. It was how poorly Tebow was throwing the ball.

Most of the Dolphins game. Most of the Lions game. Most of practice.

THE LIONS UPENDED ANY CONFIDENCE THE BRONCOS HAD IN THEIR NEW QUARTERBACK. *John Leyba, Denver Post*

With the exception of a clutch, five-minute stretch to pull out an improbable win at Miami, Tebow was not passing the eye test.

How bad was the defeat to Detroit in front of the home crowd at Sports Authority Field at Mile High?

Wrote The Denver Post's Mike Klis in his game story:

There were many other numbers as ugly as the final score. Tebow and the Broncos' offense:

• Had eight possessions of three plays or fewer.

• Were 0-for-10 on third downs before Detroit's defense allowed a couple of meaningless conversions in the fourth quarter.

• Took two delay-of-game penalties.

• Allowed seven sacks, one that resulted in a fumble returned 24 yards by Lions defensive end Cliff Avril for a touchdown.

• Early in the fourth quarter, Tebow was an unsightly 8-of-25 passing for 87 yards and an interception that was returned 100 yards for a touchdown by Lions cornerback Chris Houston.

"It's too early to say," Fox said when asked if Tebow would remain Denver's starting quarterback. "I haven't even had a shower yet, let alone looked at that tape. But we'll look at it and make changes where we see they are needed. We've definitely got to get better."

Today, Tebow's critics are beaming. From the time he was finishing up his career at Florida, NFL analysts who were former coaches, quarterbacks and players said his long throwing delivery would be a problem.

Sunday, Detroit pass rushers twice swatted the ball out of his hand as he was cocking w-a-a-a-y back to throw. On one, Avril blew past rookie right tackle Orlando Franklin, knocked the ball loose as Tebow reared to throw and returned the fumble for a touchdown.

On another Tebow sack, Lions linebacker Stephen Tulloch celebrated by falling into the prayerful "Tebowing" pose.

"It was no disrespect to Tebow," Tulloch said. "I was able to get him and had a little fun with it and decided to do some Tebowing. I saw it on websites, saw it on 'SportsCenter' and I said: 'You know what? I'm going to try it out.'"

But mocking "Tebowing" is the very definition of disrespect, isn't it?

"No, not at all," Tulloch said. "I wasn't praying. I was just having fun with it."

Later, former Broncos tight end Tony Scheffler half-mocked the Tebowing pose after catching a 1-yard touchdown pass to give the Lions a 17-3 lead late in the first half, then thought better of it and finished off his end-zone celebration by flashing the Mile High Salute.

The Roar has been restored in Detroit. Some air was let out of Tebowmania in Denver.

• • •

With Fox issuing no more than a tepid endorsement of Tebow as his quarterback, the local media enjoyed a week of splendor. This was what critics of sports journalism, many of whom were players in locker rooms of all sports, said was its purpose circa 2011: To stir debate. The days when journalism's primary responsibility was to inform? That was so 20th century. Blogs, tweets, Facebook, talk radio and other social streams – such as forums for readers to publish their comments on the bottom of news stories or analysis pieces – had changed the information game.

Good writers provoked discussion. That's always been true, at least since satirist Mark Twain captivated the nation in the late 1800s.

But provocative opinion exploded in the second decade of the 21st century. People picked up The Denver Post to read what Woody Paige, Mark Kiszla and Dave Krieger thought about Tebow through two starts.

They did not disappoint.

Wrote Kiszla in the days after the Detroit debacle and days before hotshot USC quarterback prospect Matt Barkley came to the area to play the Colorado Buffaloes:

BOULDER » Sorry, but Tim Tebow is not the answer for the Broncos.

Next.

A very real solution to what ails our local NFL franchise at quarterback is coming to Colorado for inspection, when Matt Barkley of USC plays Friday night against the Buffaloes at Folsom Field.

Let's hope Broncos executive John Elway has bought a ticket.

• • •

As it so happened, Elway and general manager Brian Xanders did take in the Trojans-Buffs game at Folsom Field. They watched Barkley throw six touchdown passes in a 42-17 victory. But a month later, Barkley announced he would return to USC for his senior season, bypassing the NFL draft in which he was all but assured of becoming a top-10 selection.

Twice in the week after the loss to the Lions and heading into the game at Oakland, The Denver Post looked at the Play Or Not To Play Tebow question.

One story was written by Broncos beat writer Jeff Legwold, who analytically viewed both sides of the argument:

There are pros and cons to every decision. Here are three of each on whether Fox should pull Tebow or stay the course:

THE LIONS' PASS RUSH KEYED ON TEBOW'S MECHANICAL WEAKNESSES AS A PASSER. *Joe Amon, The Denver Post*

TIME TO PULL TEBOW

• It's needed for the offense. The Broncos rank 27th in the 32-team NFL in yards per game and 23rd in points per game, having played two quarterbacks already. Some people think it's best to look at all three quarterbacks on the roster in game situations before the season gets completely out of hand. Brady Quinn has yet to take a snap this season.

Orton wasn't mobile enough to escape pressure, and the mobile Tebow hasn't thrown well enough to escape pressure.

The Broncos have surrendered 22 sacks in only seven games – tied for sixth-highest in the league – and rank 28th in team completion percentage. They're not moving the ball, they're not scoring and they're not winning.

• It's needed for Tebow. He may just need a break from the pressure of being Tebow – on and off the field.

His long-term development might be harmed if he's asked to play the position before he's capable. He's having difficulty reading defenses and throwing on time to the right receiver.

He and his representatives haven't done anything to pull him from the limelight, endorsements and book tours, and the Broncos put him on the cover of the season-ticket brochure even after executive John Elway and Fox said Orton was the starter. Is that best for Tebow the player?

Some in the league say it's time for Tebow's business handlers to let him work on first becoming a quarterback rather than a marketing magnet.

• It's needed for the locker room. There is a faction of the Broncos' locker room that believes Orton was unfairly singled out for the team's struggles. Champ Bailey, Mario Hag-

WILL TO WIN: CHAPTER 8

gan and André Goodman have said so. Professionalism demands a player struggling such as Tebow go to the bench, quarterback or not.

Rookie Von Miller, the team's sack leader, was benched against the Chargers after making two major assignment mistakes. Other players have gone to the bench after fewer mistakes than Tebow has made in two starts.

STAYING WITH TEBOW
• You can't change quarterbacks like you change shirts. Enough is enough. The team already has tweaked its playbook significantly trying to adjust from Orton to Tebow.

To make another adjustment for another QB only sets them further back.

Tebow has yet to develop an on-field rapport with the receivers. The offensive line is struggling to block for Tebow when it doesn't know where he's going to be as he moves around behind the line of scrimmage.

There is little on-field chemistry. And unless the Broncos are prepared to go back to Orton, that would take even more time to develop if Quinn were put in the lineup.

• It's been two games. If the task is to find out, without a doubt, where Tebow stands as the potential long-

WHEN CHAMP BAILEY SAID, "IF YOU DON'T HAVE THE TALENT FOR THIS LEAGUE, IT'S HARD TO PLAY," YOU CAN BE SURE PEOPLE PAID ATTENTION.
Hyoung Chang, The Denver Post

term starter for the Broncos, then an improbable victory over a winless team and one horrible afternoon against a playoff-bound team is not a representative sample. More time is needed to see if Tebow can change some of the things that need changing when the game-day heat is on.

• It's time to just play. The Broncos have only one playoff victory in the past 12 seasons. They haven't even been to the playoffs since the 2005 season. They were 4-12 last season.

This isn't one of the NFL's elite teams trying to recover from a small stumble. This is a franchise that is far closer to the league's bottom than to the league's top. It's time for everybody, from the top down, to just dig in and play the hand they have.

Help is not on the way. They won't get another swing at free agency until March, and the draft isn't until April. Quit looking for someone to jump in with a life preserver.

As Fox put it: "Part of the team (concept) is, especially when things aren't going well, you're best off looking at yourself and seeing what you can do better and not be so concerned about what somebody else is doing."

• • •

Then there was the write-off between Paige and Krieger. Paige, who hitched his literary wagon to Tebow the minute the Gator great was drafted by the Broncos, offered compelling reasons for the Broncos to stay patient.

Krieger, whose analysis often digs below the surface of an issue until it scrapes its roots, offered reasons for benching Tebow if for no other reason than for the kid's own good.

Stay with Tebow? Paige: Yes!
History says it's too early to pull Tebow, 2-3 through five starts.

ESPN analyst Trent Dilfer, 1-4 record, two touchdowns, nine interceptions, would be the QB on Ravens' Super Bowl-winning team.

Southern football icon and No. 2 pick overall, Archie Manning, 2-2-1, 40-of-86 passing, five touchdowns, five interceptions, 10.9 rating in one game as Saints rookie, father of two NFL quarterbacks.

The Colts' (injured) Peyton Manning, No. 1 pick, 1-4, four touchdowns, 12 interceptions, would win one Super Bowl.

The Giants' Eli Manning, No. 1 pick (traded from Chargers following

> "Remember he's not ready (whether) you like it or not. No comparison whatsoever. No other QB in the history of the NFL has been given a pass with this style of play. Period!"
>
> **Kordell Stewart,** former NFL player

88 THE DENVER POST

AFTER A DISASTROUS OUTING AGAINST DETROIT, TEBOW WAS ON A SHORT LEASH. *Tim Rasmussen, The Denver Post*

draft), 0-5, three touchdowns, seven interceptions, would win one Super Bowl.

The Packers' Aaron Rodgers, 2-3 as starter, finally, in fourth season, nine touchdowns, four interceptions, would win one Super Bowl.

Fox analyst Terry Bradshaw, 2-3, one touchdown, eight interceptions, 41-of-100 passing, would win four Super Bowls, Hall of Famer.

ESPN commentator Steve Young, 1-4 with Tampa Bay, three touchdowns, eight interceptions, would be 49ers' starting quarterback on one Super Bowl-winning team, Hall of Famer.

Fox analyst Troy Aikman, 0-5, three touchdowns, eight interceptions, won three Super Bowls with Cowboys, Hall of Famer.

Joe Montana, 1-4, six touchdowns, four interceptions, won four Super Bowls with 49ers, Hall of Famer.

Brett Favre, 2-3, six touchdowns, two interceptions, won one Super Bowl with Packers.

• • •

On Paige went, using the five-game statistical documents of Sam Bradford, Cam Newton, Michael Vick, Colt McCoy, Ryan Fitzpatrick.

And Johnny Unitas.

Paige then rounded third with his column and headed for home.

Then, there is: Tim Tebow, 2-3 as Broncos starter, seven touchdowns, four interceptions.

In five starts, Tebow has passed for 984 yards, rushed for 321 yards and completed 48.3 percent of his passes. In comparison, Elway (knocked out of his first game, replaced in the second half of his fifth game) passed for 420 yards, rushed for 41 yards, completed 45.8 percent and was 2-3 with one touchdown, five interceptions.

The Broncos did not give up on

WILL TO WIN: CHAPTER 8

QUARTERBACKS COACH ADAM GASE WORKED WITH TEBOW AND OFFENSIVE COORDINATOR MIKE McCOY TO INSTALL THE READ-OPTION OFFENSE, WHICH WOULD TAKE INTO ACCOUNT THE STRENGTH OF THEIR QUARTERBACK. *John Leyba, The Denver Post*

Elway then. The Broncos must not give up on Tebow now.

•••

That's not what Krieger thought. Stay with Tebow? Krieger: No!

It comes down to this: You can't stink it up as badly as the Broncos' offense has for seven of its last eight quarters if you're a young quarterback trying to earn a job.

You can't sandwich six three-and-outs around a turnover for an opponent touchdown if you're making a case that you're ready to run an NFL offense.

That was Tim Tebow's body of work for most of the second and third quarters last Sunday against Detroit. Today's effort at Oakland cannot resemble that if he wants his audition as Broncos starting quarterback to continue next week.

When the team went nowhere in its first five games under the direction of veteran Kyle Orton, I was all for giving Tebow a chance. But a chance is not the same thing as a free pass no matter how bad it gets.

"You can be as competitive and have as much heart as possible, but if you don't have the talent for this league, it's hard to play," all-pro cornerback Champ Bailey said after last week's 45-10 loss.

Bailey went on to praise Tebow's work ethic, but that first part should have been, and probably was, a red flag to John Elway and John Fox. It is one thing for outsiders to suggest your quarterback can't play. It is quite another when it's your own players.

None of this is to suggest Tebow won't ever be able to play quarterback in the NFL. It is only to suggest, as Kordell Stewart did last week, that he can't now.

"Remember he's not ready (whether) you like it or not. No comparison whatsoever. No other QB in the history of the NFL has been given a pass with this style of play. Period!

"Many QBs coming out of high school, college (have) been converted. But Tebow's the exception to the rule? No! He needs to sit like Steve McNair, go to Canada like Warren Moon, play another sport like Charlie Ward."

If he is great, let him demonstrate it today in Oakland by beginning to rebuild the Broncos' credibility with a competitive game.

If he's not, the organization should end the madness and give Brady Quinn a shot next week in Kansas City before Elway and Fox lose the locker room.

•••

In a way, Paige and Krieger were both right. Fox would stick with Tebow, as Paige suggested. But Fox also had pulled the quarterback from the conventional-style offense, as Krieger requested.

While every Woody, Dave, Dick and Tom debated, little did anyone outside the Broncos' meeting rooms know that besides putting Tebow on notice, Fox was also rebuilding his offense to suit his quarterback's skills. Specifically, Fox told offensive coordinator Mike McCoy and quarterbacks coach Adam Gase to install the read-option offense that Tebow ran at the University of Florida.

They had given Tebow designed runs before, of course. But this was an option where Tebow was to read the defensive end. If the defensive end or outside linebacker crashed towards him, Tebow had the option to pull the ball out of Willis McGahee's stomach and beat the edge defender around end.

If the end or linebacker was sitting back, Tebow could stuff it in McGahee's cradling arms.

Like most of the world's best ideas, it was a simple but brilliant concept. The week after the loss to the Lions, Fox unveiled the new read-option offense against the Raiders in Oakland.

USING A READ-OPTION OFFENSE, THE BRONCOS ROLLED UP 299 YARDS RUSHING IN A 38-24 WIN AT OAKLAND. *John Leyba, The Denver Post*

All that happened next for the Broncos was a six-game winning streak.

Wrote Mike Klis in his game account in The Denver Post of the Broncos' 38-24 win at Oakland:

OAKLAND » Football on Sundays has become an aerial show.

Knowing Tim Tebow is not a conventional Sunday quarterback, the Broncos' coaching staff came up with an innovative idea against the Oakland Raiders:

They brought football back to Saturdays.

Using a read-option running attack that hasn't been seen in the NFL since … since … since when? Since before helmets had face masks?

Anyway, the Broncos defeated the Oakland Raiders 38-24 at Overstock Coliseum here Sunday in an AFC West game that was widely characterized as an upset.

But the surprise was on the edge of the Raiders' defensive front that kept crashing inside as Tebow kept the ball around end. With Tebow either keeping the ball or handing

> "We've definitely made adjustments. We've been in the process of adjusting for the last three weeks. **It's a different style, but it can be effective.**"
>
> **John Fox,** on installing a read-option offense for the Oakland game

off to Willis McGahee – Tebow had the option to choose which one – the Broncos amassed 299 yards rushing. In the Broncos' best running game since the year 2000, Tebow, the quarterback, had 118 yards rushing and McGahee, the running back, had 163.

That's 281 yards rushing between them. Just two months ago, the Broncos BT – Before Tebow – had 38 yards rushing in a season-opening loss to the Raiders in Denver.

The last time Raiders quarterback Carson Palmer, who has been in the NFL since he was the No. 1 overall draft pick in 2003, had seen a read-option offense?

"I think it was college," he said.

Sometimes, innovation is having the guts to do what has already been done. Let the rest of the NFL carry on with its Aaron Rodgers, Drew Brees, Tom Brady and Manning brothers.

Tebow's skills, it's been argued, are for another day. In his three starts this year, the Broncos are averaging an incredible 233.3 yards rushing per game.

He is arguably the greatest Saturday quarterback who ever played. While operating the read-option, spread offense at the University of Florida, Tebow was the first sophomore to win a Heisman Trophy, and he nearly won it two more times. He was part of two national championship teams.

Turns out, what's old to college ball is new to the NFL. "That's hard to defend," said Broncos cornerback Champ Bailey, who picked a good time for his first two interceptions of the season. "Especially when you have a quarterback who's as explosive as Tebow is. Tebow doesn't get enough credit for his explosiveness. I know he would love to sharpen up his passing, but at the same time he's running the ball extremely well."

Come to think of it, the pass-heavy Sunday league does get a little monotonous, don't you think? Broncos offensive coordinator Mike McCoy did. So, on several plays, McCoy designed plays that gave Tebow the option: From the shotgun, the lefty quarterback could either hand off to McGahee or keep it himself and run around end.

"There were a couple of times when I was supposed to give it to him," Tebow said, as he finished putting on his tie in front of his locker. "But I thought I could beat the guy around end, so I kept it."

Holy J.C. Watts, Dee Dowis and Tommie Frazier. Tebow's dual-threat game complemented McGahee, who, less than two weeks removed from surgery to repair a broken right hand, had touchdown runs of 60 yards, which occurred on the last play of the third quarter that tied the game 24-24, and 24 yards just before the two-minute warning that capped the win.

Tebow and McGahee became the Broncos' first quarterback-running back combination to each rush for 100 yards in the same game since Norris Weese and Otis Armstrong pulled off the feat in a Dec. 12, 1976, game.

"It's a tribute to our coaches," Fox said of the throwback-to-Saturday offense. "We've definitely made adjustments. We've been in the process of adjusting for the last three weeks (since Tebow replaced Kyle Orton as the starting quarterback). It's a different style, but it can be effective."

Tebow not only ran the Raiders silly around end, he threw touchdown passes of 27 yards to Eric Decker and 26 yards to Eddie Royal.

Through the suffocating Orton-Tebow debate, through the Tebow-is-a-winner/Tebow-can't-play discussion, through losses of 26 points on the road (to Green Bay) and 35 points at home (last week to Detroit), the Broncos have reached the halfway point of the 2011 season in an improbable position: one game out of the AFC West lead.

The San Diego Chargers, Kansas City Chiefs and Raiders, all of whom lost at home Sunday, are 4-4. The Tebow-led Broncos are 3-5. The AFC West race has become a neck-and-neck crawl.

Let Andrew Luck worry about playing for the college national championship. The Broncos will start the second half of their season next Sunday in Kansas City knowing no one but Tebow will be leading their team.

Asked if he was ready to commit to Tebow as his starting quarterback next week at Kansas City, Fox this time did not have to use the old "need to first take a shower and watch film" excuse.

WELL INTO THE FOURTH QUARTER AT KANSAS CITY, TEBOW WAS 1-OF-7 PASSING FOR 13 YARDS. *John Leyba, The Denver Post*

"Yes, I can," he said.

For the first time in his NFL career, Tebow was challenged with his starting job this past week. That he responded with an always solid, sometimes brilliant performance didn't surprise anyone who knows him well.

"Honestly, I put that pressure on myself more than anybody else," Tebow said. "To try to improve and ultimately get a victory no matter how it looks. That was a special one."

• • •

What Klis failed to mention in his review of the Raiders game was that after a 29-yard completion to Demaryius Thomas with 6:38 remaining in the third quarter, Tebow did not attempt another pass.

The Broncos finished that game with 19 consecutive runs. The "four corners" finish became significant when the aerial drought crashed the next week against Kansas City.

Incredibly, preposterously, Tebow reached halftime against the Chiefs with zero pass completions. And a 10-0 lead. The Broncos ended up winning 17-10 at Arrowhead Stadium,

> "If this didn't work, we would have been saying the same thing to ourselves inside the building: 'Hey, what were we thinking?'"
>
> **John Fox,** after beating Kansas City

but the most memorable numerical sequence was this: 55 runs, 8 passes. Only 2 of those 8 passes were completions.

And to repeat, the Broncos won.

Wrote Klis in his Denver Post gamer:
The score was not indicative of the decade. The Broncos ran the ball 55 times even though their top two running backs, Willis McGahee and Knowshon Moreno, suffered first-quarter injuries and did not return.

No problem. The Broncos "opened" their playbook and called 30 rushing attempts for No. 3 tailback Lance Ball.

Tebow took zero completions for zero passing yards into the halftime locker room. Oh, and a 10-0 lead.

Tebow ran the ball. Ran for a touchdown on his first possession, even. He pitched the ball. He handed off. He faked a few passes before handing off.

But he did not complete a pass. Not until more than 12 minutes were gone in the third quarter, he didn't.

One of the most memorable match-ups between Woody Hayes-coached Ohio State and Bo Schembechler-led Michigan was a 10-10 tie in 1973. Hayes, who coached until he was fired for punching a Clemson player in the throat in a 1978 bowl game and died in 1987, passed for zero yards in that Michigan game. Hayes' Buckeyes were ranked No. 1 in the country, and in their biggest game of the year, they pass for zero yards.

Which ordinarily would seem incredible even today, except Tebow just went a full game's worth without a passing yard, too.

In the Broncos' 38-24 win at Oakland last week, Tebow threw his last pass, a 29-yard completion to Demaryius Thomas, with 6:38 remaining in the third quarter.

The Broncos finished that game with 19 consecutive plays without a pass attempt. There was one sack in there, which is not a rushing attempt. But whatever. In the game here against the Chiefs, the Broncos ran 14 plays in the first quarter. All running plays.

In all, the Broncos ran 33 consecutive plays without a pass attempt – 32 runs and one sack – until Tebow opened the second quarter against the Chiefs by heaving a deep incompletion downfield.

"I'll leave those statistics to you guys," said Broncos coach John "Don't Call Me Woody Hayes" Fox. "The statistic that is important in (the locker room) is winning. This game is only fun when you win."

Tebow was 0-for-5 with 3:58 remaining in the third quarter when he flipped a safe, short pass to Matt Willis for a 13-yard gain.

Those wild-and-crazy Broncos play-callers.

Add it up and Tebow went four quarters and nearly three minutes of game clock – and about three hours short of seven full days – without a completion.

No matter, the Broncos scored a touchdown and field goal from their first three possessions to go up 10-0. And they had the perfect four-corners offense to protect it.

"10-0 was huge," said Casey Wiegmann, the Chiefs and former Broncos center. "After that, the game was: Eat up the clock and (Britton) Colquitt punting the ball to the 15."

The Chiefs' offense, frustrated by all the time it spent watching Tebow hog the ball, finally put together a scoring drive by using the more conventional methods of mixing in the pass and the run in the third quarter.

It remained 10-7 with less than seven minutes remaining in the game, at which point Tebow was 1-of-7 passing for 13 yards.

"Don't get me wrong," Fox said as he walked to the team bus, "we've got to get better in the passing game."

And then, as only Tebow can seemingly do in the fourth quarter, the lefty whipped a beautiful 56-yard touchdown pass to Eric Decker, who beat the lulled Chiefs' secondary to sleep.

It was Decker's only catch of the game. Tebow sat on his 2-of-8 passing game from there. Tebow had himself a rushing touchdown, a passing touchdown, a 102.6 rating and a 3-1 record as a starting quarterback. All three of those wins are on the road.

"I've got to make a few better throws," Tebow said. "We'll continue to get better. But overall, it worked out because we got a win. And we've got to continue to find a way to do that."

The win lifted the Broncos' overall record to 4-5 and into a second-place tie with the Chiefs and San Diego Chargers in the AFC West. Oakland

ONCE TEBOW READ THE JETS LINEBACKER, HE SCOOTED AROUND THE END AND HEADED FOR THE END ZONE.

John Leyba, The Denver Post

John Leyba, The Denver Post

Tim Rasmussen, The Denver Post

> "Put in this offense and some quarterbacks in the league would look at you like you had three heads. **Tebow feeds off it.**"
>
> **John Fox,** on his quarterback's ability to run the read-option offense

leads the division with a 5-4 mark.

The Broncos, easily the NFL's top rushing team at 228.8 yards per game since Tebow became a starter, have just run their way back into playoff contention.

Is this really how the Broncos are going to play in John Elway's first year as football operations boss?

• • •

The new offense – or old offense, depending on one's point of view – completely altered the perception of Fox. Long considered an ultraconservative coach by today's NFL pass-happy standards, Fox now had the best of both worlds, a running game that made him look like a genius.

Wrote Denver Post columnist Mark Kiszla in the shortened period between the Broncos' win at Kansas City on Nov. 13 and upcoming game Nov. 17 against the New York Jets before a Thursday night prime-time audience:

Not to suggest the NFL is rocket science, but building a playoff contender with Tim Tebow at quarterback is like flying to the moon in a space shuttle made from Lego blocks.

What on heaven or earth could Broncos coach John Fox have been thinking when he took the big gamble of trying to win pro games by putting complete faith in the run and declaring "pass" a four-letter word?

Good question.

"If this didn't work," Fox told me Tuesday, "we would have been saying the same thing to ourselves inside the building: 'Hey, what were we thinking?'"

If the Broncos somehow make the playoffs, Fox deserves a bigger trophy than coach of the year.

How about a Nobel Prize for inventing this hot-tub time machine that Tebow and the Broncos have ridden back to AFC West title contention?

Tebow is an undeniable, storybook winner, with his legend only writ larger since he took over as starting quarterback of a hopeless, last-place team, then rallied Denver to three victories in four games.

But maybe the real football miracle worker here is Fox.

The Broncos' magical victory tour has rolled through Miami, Oakland and Kansas City with a quarterback the league openly discredits as a passer. The big mouth of New York Jets coach Rex Ryan was the latest to risk the wrath of Tebow Nation by disrespecting the young quarterback.

"Obviously, going against Denver, their priority is to run the football, and you have to stop it," said Ryan, doing a little baiting of the Broncos in advance of a showdown Thursday night. "You don't have to worry about playing pass defense or rushing the passer, because they won't throw it."

OK, now Ryan has really offended anybody with a No. 15 jersey hanging in the closet. Doesn't Ryan realize Denver is a town of Little League mothers and fathers who have adopted Tebow as their favorite son? Any slight, real or perceived, will not be tolerated.

For example, there's the wacky conspiracy theory that won't die. Broncos executive John Elway and Fox secretly want Tebow to fail, because he was a first-round draft choice of Josh McDaniels, generally considered the biggest knucklehead ever to roam the Denver sideline.

"That doesn't make much sense to me. Like buying a Ferrari and pouring sugar in the gas tank," Fox told New York media during a conference call.

And then there's this cockamamie notion: Despite ripping up his playbook in the middle of the season, asking NFL athletes to turn the clock back 60 years to drop the forward pass like a bad habit and doing everything short of treating his QB to an ice-cream cone after every victory, we are supposed to believe Fox has been slow to go all-in with his support of Tebow?

"No knock against anybody else, but the quarterback we have now likes this stuff. He has a bigger body. Running is one of this guy's strengths," Fox said. "Put in this offense and some quarterbacks in the league would look at you like you had three heads. Tebow feeds off it. He likes the physical part of football, and it's a little bit unique. He can pass. But this is an ability (Tebow) has that most quarterbacks don't have in this league."

By running straight through conventional wisdom, Tebow is making his coach look like a genius.

"It's not like we were setting the world on fire. I mean, we were sitting there with a 1-4 record," Fox said. "We had to find out if something else could work."

• • •

Next up were the Jets. And Tebow did it again, finishing off another fourth-quarter comeback by breaking containment from the pocket and

WITH ANOTHER LAST-MINUTE WIN IN HAND, TEBOW GAVE THE MILE HIGH SALUTE TO THE HOMETOWN FANS. *Joe Amon, The Denver Post*

scrambling for a game-winning, 20-yard touchdown run with 58 seconds remaining.

The Broncos had won their third in a row since installing the read-option offense for Tebow and had evened their overall record at 5-5.

The day after their victory over the Jets, Fox lamented his comment to Darlington.

"I screwed up," Fox said. "What bothers me about that is I love Tim Tebow. How can you not? I'm his biggest fan."

That Fox was Tebow's biggest fan was difficult to believe. Not because there was doubt about whether Fox was warming up to the guy. It's just that the claim "Tebow's biggest fan" is like saying chocolate ice cream is the best dessert: There are just so many to choose from.

Tebow fans were everywhere. He captivated the patrons at Yesterday's Bar & Grill in Clifton, N.J. He became part of a Texas governor's Republican primary campaign for U.S. president. People were custom ordering Broncos No. 15 jerseys with "Jesus" on the back nameplate.

People across the land were "Tebowing."

Tebowmania was spreading from its roots in Florida and then Colorado, to across the northern border in Canada and overseas in Korea.

If John Fox was Tebow's biggest fan, he was not without enormous competition.

WILL TO WIN: CHAPTER 9

RESPECT HIM OR NOT, CHANCES ARE PRETTY GOOD THAT YOU HAVE HEARD OF HIM

On Sunday afternoons in New York City, Sidebar has become home away from home for Colorado transplants living in Manhattan. It was just outside Sidebar, an upscale bar near Union Square, on the evening of Oct. 23, 2011, that a pop-culture phenomenon was born.

Jared Kleinstein, a 24-year-old Denver native, had just watched the Broncos' thrilling 18-15 overtime victory over Miami in Tim Tebow's first start of the season.

A mixed crowd of die-hard Broncos fans, such as Kleinstein, and new Broncos converts – you could spot them wearing the royal blue No. 15 jerseys, the University of Florida variety – cheered as Tebow led a frantic fourth-quarter comeback, engineering two touchdown drives (one with a two-point conversion) to force overtime.

"No offense to (Rockies star Troy Tulowitzki), but the entire bar was doing the 'Tu-lo!' chant to Tebow," Kleinstein said. "It's contagious. Love him or hate him, but Tebow fever is contagious."

As Matt Prater's 52-yard field goal sailed through the uprights in overtime, the bar erupted in celebration. Kleinstein was fixated on the television, drawn to the image of Tebow kneeling on the sideline in prayer as the rest of his teammates engaged in wild celebration.

When Kleinstein and his buddies left the bar a short time later, he suggested they mimic Tebow's prayer pose on the sidewalk on East 15th Street. Kleinstein

TEBOW MAY HAVE FIRST GRABBED THE NATION'S ATTENTION WHEN HE WON THE HEISMAN. *Kelly Kline, The Associated Press*

WILL TO WIN: CHAPTER 9

> "I don't know what to think about that because **I don't know where people's hearts are.**"
>
> Tim Tebow

posted the picture on his Facebook page upon returning home, and his online friends went wild. Inspired, Kleinstein dubbed the term "Tebowing," gave it a definition ("to get down on a knee and start praying, even if everyone else around you is doing something completely different") and purchased the web address Tebowing.com.

Within days, Tebowing had gone viral.

By Thursday, Oct. 28, it had reached Dove Valley. Broncos rookie linebacker Von Miller, one of the team's most active Twitter users, swiped one of Tebow's orange No. 15 practice jerseys and Tebowed in the team's equipment room.

"Goofball," Tebow said the next day, laughing.

Miller's picture directed Tebow's attention to Kleinstein's website, where random people from around the world had begun uploading their own Tebowing photos.

Tebow quickly picked a favorite: a young cancer patient in Tebow's prayer pose while hooked up to a chemotherapy machine. "Tebowing while chemoing," the boy wrote. (That child, Joey Norris, was Tebow's guest at Sports Authority Field at Mile High for the regular-season finale against Kansas City as part of the Tebow Foundation's Wish 15 program.)

Kleinstein said he started the website as a tribute to Tebow. It was not meant to mock Tebow, the quarterback's strong Christian faith or the act of prayer, Kleinstein said.

Tebow was flattered.

"It's not my job to see people's reasons behind it, but I know (of a kid) with cancer that tweeted me, 'Tebowing while I'm chemoing' — how cool is that?" Tebow said. "That's worth it right now. If that gives him any encouragement or puts a smile on his face or gives him encouragement to pray, that's completely awesome."

Tebowmania with the Broncos began April 22, 2010, when the team's then-coach and player personnel boss, Josh McDaniels, surprised the NFL by taking the passing-challenged left-hander in the first round.

Most draft pundits rated Tebow as a third-round talent, maybe fourth round, because he was a project who would need two years to develop.

When McDaniels took Tebow No. 25 overall, Tebowmania exploded. Although Tebow was a Bronco for only eight full days in April, his No. 15 Broncos jersey became the No. 1 seller for the month on NFLShop.com. Donovan McNabb's new jersey with the Washington Redskins was No. 2, followed by Drew Brees, Peyton Manning and Brett Favre. We know what you're thinking: "What have those guys done?"

Two months into the 2010 regular season, through Halloween, Tebow had not yet thrown an NFL pass. Yet he was still No. 1 in NFL jersey sales.

By then Favre had thrown 10,000 more passes and 500 more touchdowns than Tebow. But hey, Brett, mind getting out of the way?

The roots of Tebowmania were well established before Kleinstein got his idea. But there's no doubt that two weeks later, when the Broncos began a six-game winning streak, Tebowmania reached new, unfathomable heights.

It wasn't just Tebowing, though celebrities (such as actress Dianna Agron from the television show "Glee") and superstar athletes (such as NBA center Dwight Howard and Olympic skier Lindsey Vonn) joined the craze. From early November until just before Christmas, Tebow was arguably the biggest sports celebrity in the country. He was bigger than Denver; bigger than the NFL. Tebow's fame transcended sports and seeped into American culture at large.

Bigger than? There was a time in November when people would go to the NFLShop.com website, order a No. 15 Broncos jersey, and instead of putting Tebow's name on the back, or their own name, they would customize their order by putting "JESUS" as the name.

No. 15 and Jesus.

Wrote Mike Klis in the Denver Post:

It is written that Jesus sits at the right hand of the Father.

Anyone ever wonder why Tim Tebow was born left-handed?

There are some Tebow zealots who may not think it's a coincidence. Even as theologians debate whether it is the archangel Gabriel who sits at the left hand of heaven's throne, there are Tebow fans who believe the Broncos' starting quarterback is worthy of the highest of standings.

First there was "Tebowing," with fans kneeling in prayer in places

"TEBOWING" BECAME A WORLDWIDE HIT. LINDSEY VONN STRIKES THE POSE. *Andy Cross, The Denver Post*

outside a church setting, as Tebow did on the Denver sideline in Miami after Matt Prater kicked his winning field goal in overtime Oct. 23.

Now, Broncos fans are going a step further, customizing their No. 15 jerseys with the name "JESUS" on the back.

The "JESUS" jersey has created a little more controversy than "Tebowing" because it has been viewed by some Christians as a transgression of the first commandment that prohibits idolatry.

But others say that instead of the more common "John 3:16," fans are honoring their faith in the Son of God by using the jersey of Tebow, an unabashed believer, as sort of a billboard.

"I don't know what to think about that because I don't know where people's hearts are," Tebow said. "It's important to not judge without knowing their hearts. If their heart is to honor the Lord, then it's a good thing. Only God can judge because only God knows what's truly in a person's heart."

As with all things Tebow, the

WILL TO WIN: CHAPTER 9

A NATIONAL BOOK TOUR, INCLUDING AN APPEARANCE AT THE TATTERED COVER IN DENVER TO PROMOTE HIS BOOK "THROUGH MY EYES," KEPT TEBOW IN THE LIMELIGHT DESPITE THE NFL LOCKOUT. *Craig F. Walker, The Denver Post*

"JESUS" jersey has grown from one by one to a nationwide fad. All anyone has to do is go to NFLshop.com and customize the name and number they want on their team jersey.

With a current 15 percent discount on customizing the jersey, No. 15 "JESUS" jerseys can be had for $94.99 apiece.

• • •

Tebow is also a best-selling author (his autobiography "Through My Eyes" climbed to No. 4 on The New York Times list for nonfiction in the last week of December); a big-money pitch man (with endorsements for Nike, Jockey, EAS video games and FRS nutritional supplements); and a bona fide pop-culture icon.

This was never more evident than on Saturday, Dec. 17, when NBC's "Saturday Night Live" parodied Tebow in a comedy sketch, featuring a postgame locker-room scene interrupted by the appearance of Jesus Christ ("Just a quick visit," quipped actor Jason Sudekis, draped in full Jesus garb).

It took awhile but Tebow did eventually see the skit on the Internet. He was spoofed as naive and gullible. In describing his reaction, he chose his words carefully. "I did see it, but I didn't want to finish watching it," he said. "I feel like I can laugh at myself pretty well, but ... It's all right. At least they are talking about it, talking about Jesus."

Tebowmania was out of control. In the days leading up to the Dec. 18 home game against New England (whose quarterback, Tom Brady, has fame also transcendent of the NFL), Tebow and politics collided.

Republican presidential candidate Rick Perry, in his opening statements, said he wanted to be the "Tim Tebow of the Iowa caucuses."

Perry said:

"There are a lot of folks that said Tim Tebow wasn't going to be a very good NFL quarterback. There are people that stood up and said, well, he doesn't have the right throwing mechanisms, or he doesn't – you know, he is not playing the game right. You know, he won two national championships, and that looked pretty good. We're the national champions in job creation back in Texas. But am I ready for the next level? Let me tell you – I hope I am the Tim Tebow of the Iowa caucuses."

Tebow was famous long before he arrived in Denver.

As one of the top high school recruits in the state of Florida in 2005, Tebow and his Nease High School teammates played in a nationally televised game at Alabama powerhouse Hoover.

He arrived at the University of Florida in January 2006 with the makings of a cult hero. He played sporadically as a freshman that fall – in short-yardage packages or as a change-of-pace from starter Chris Leak – but immediately became a fan favorite and the most famous Gator on a team that included a dozen future NFL players.

In 2007, his first season as Florida's starter, he emerged as a national star, becoming the first sophomore to win the Heisman Trophy. On the ESPN broadcast the night of the Heisman ceremony, the Tebow family first told the story – in such a public forum, at least – of Tebow's difficult birth.

Tebow's fame only grew in 2008 as Florida won its second Southeastern Conference title (behind a Tebow-led fourth-quarter comeback against Alabama) and second national championship (against Oklahoma) in three years. Tebow opted to return to Gainesville for a final season in 2009, and he ended his career (with a win in the Sugar Bowl) as perhaps the most decorated collegiate player ever. Certainly the most publicized.

That context is important when examining the current state of

TEBOW HAD BECOME ACCUSTOMED TO TAKING THE LEAD – IN HIGH SCHOOL, COLLEGE AND NOW IN THE NFL.

Autumn Cruz, Orlando Sentinel

Phil Sandlin, The Associated Press

John Leyba, The Denver Post

> "I told the guys, 'Hey, guys, I appreciate the crowd support, but I'm here for you guys. **I want you guys to believe in me.'**"
>
> Tim Tebow

Tebowmania. In his four years at Florida, Tebow developed a rabid, and intensely loyal, fan base. He was beloved by old-school football fans for the way he played the game – tough, and with passion – and by the casual fan, and even non-fan, for his good-guy persona.

This fan base followed him to Denver, and – after the Broncos' 4-12 season in 2010 (3-10 with Kyle Orton) – those Tebowites joined a Broncos base that was ready for change.

It helped Tebow's cause, certainly, that he was not forgotten during the NFL lockout. In fact, he was among the most visible players in the spring and summer of 2011, thanks to a national book tour to promote the May release of his autobiography. He sold out book signings in Denver, Colorado Springs, Jacksonville, Orlando and Gainesville. In Denver, the most devoted Tebow fans camped outside The Tattered Cover bookstore in Lower Downtown for the chance to be at the front of the signing line. First in line was Erin Engel, a 21-year-old nursing student from Littleton.

"I grew up in Southeast Asia, in Vietnam and Thailand, doing missionary work, and I was supposed to be aborted, so we have weird things in common," said Engel. "I was totally compelled. He's an amazing role model for everybody, and I think God has blessed him immensely with his talent and his platform."

She was beaming – and blushing – as she walked away.

"He's even better looking in real life," Engel said.

As the book tour continued, Tebow appeared on late-night shows "The Daily Show with Jon Stewart" and "Jimmy Kimmel Live," and did guest spots for Fox News and MSNBC.

He also taped an appearance on the NBC reality show "The Biggest Loser," presented an award at the ESPY Awards in late July (with Colorado-based skier Lindsey Vonn, who has since become a family friend), and was the subject of an hour-long documentary about his pre-draft journey. That documentary, filmed and produced by the son of his father's closest friend, aired on ESPN in January 2011 and was released on DVD in November.

So, by the time the NFL lockout ended in late July, Broncos fans – and Tebow fans, especially – were ready for Tebow Time.

When that didn't happen, when Kyle Orton wasn't traded, when Orton won the quarterback competition handily in training camp and was named the starter for the opener, Tebowmaniacs turned angry.

Fans at Sports Authority Field at Mile High chanted for Tebow in the Sept. 12 season opener, a 23-20 loss to Oakland. After the game, John Fox told the media he did not hear them.

In coming weeks, it would be hard to ignore the growing groundswell to play Tebow, from the chatter on talk radio to newspaper columnists pining for him to a billboard in Denver imploring Fox to "PLAY TEBOW!!"

When Tebow finally got his first start, in Game 6 at Miami, the Dolphins incredulously honored him. Nat Moore, a Dolphins executive who was a former wide receiver for the Dolphins and Florida Gators, decided to honor Florida's 2008 national championship team on the day that team's quarterback, Tebow, came to town with the Broncos.

How can an NFL team stoop so low as to come up with a promotion that essentially honors the visiting quarterback? A Dolphins organization that struggles every week to sell out their home stadium, that's who.

Tebow alone generated estimates of 5,000 to 10,000 in extra ticket sales.

Wrote Mike Klis in his review of that game:

It created an odd crowd environment. In the first half, Dolphins defensive end Jason Taylor exhorted the crowd to continue with their "Tebow Sucks" chants. In the fourth quarter, as Tebow was doing his Tebow Thing, the crowd was chanting, "Te-bow! Te-bow!"

"I try not to pay attention to it, but you do hear it," Tebow said. "Kupe (right guard Chris Kuper) said something to me about the crowd in the huddle before our first drive. I told the guys, 'Hey, guys, I appreciate the crowd support, but I'm here for you guys. I want you guys to believe in me.'"

• • •

Is this guy for real? Tebowmaniacs bought in. So did those covering Tebowmania. In early December, ESPN devoted a whole midday hour

WHETHER THE GAMES WERE PLAYED AT HOME OR ON THE ROAD, TEBOWMANIA KNEW NO LIMITS. GATOR NATION GATHERED IN MIAMI TO HONOR THEIR FAVORITE SON. HE DID NOT DISAPPOINT. *Hans Deryk, The Associated Press*

Joe Amon, The Denver Post

Steve Nehf, The Denver Post

WILL TO WIN: CHAPTER 9

> "People can tell me they're tired of Tim Tebow, but that's not what the ratings say. When we talk about Tim Tebow, the ratings go up."
>
> **Jamie Horowitz,** the coordinating producer for "First Take" and "SportsNation"

of its flagship show "SportsCenter" to cover only Tebow. The morning debate show on the sports network, "First Take," was "ground zero" for all things Tebow, said Richard Deitsch, media columnist for Sports Illustrated.

"The one thing that I find interesting is, to me, the polarization of Tebow as a subject has been amplified by the media, where you have this faux story line where people have to be either pro- or anti-Tebow," Deitsch said. "That makes for very big ratings. Tebow has been the defining argument on ESPN."

"First Take" has produced its highest ratings in the five-year history of the program since October. It is no coincidence that those shows coincide with Tebow's takeover. "First Take" commentator Skip Bayless banged the drum for Tebow for months – and freely criticizes anyone he thinks is getting in Tebow's way (John Elway, Brandon Lloyd, Eric Decker and John Fox have been among Bayless' favorite targets).

"It's the debate element of it," said Jamie Horowitz, the coordinating producer for "First Take" and "SportsNation." "It's not that it isn't a compelling narrative. He is a TV phenomenon, a Favre-like status when it comes to TV. The thing that's most amazing is that each week has only reinforced each side's passion. The highest-rated episode was Dec. 6. I e-mailed Skip on Sunday night and said to him, 'Can we do the first 25 minutes of the show on Tebow? Are there enough angles?' He wrote back and said, 'We can do all two hours.' People can tell me they're tired of Tim Tebow, but that's not what the ratings say. When we talk about Tim Tebow, the ratings go up."

The television coverage reached its apex with the Broncos' home game against New England on Dec. 18. CBS, initially scheduled to broadcast the game, and NBC, home of Sunday Night Football, fought for three days for the right to show the game. NBC wanted to "flex" the Patriots-Broncos game into its lineup. CBS, with the support of the Patriots and owner Bob Kraft, and the San Diego Chargers, who wanted their home game against Baltimore to remain in prime time, fought hard to retain the game. Ultimately, CBS won.

When overnight ratings were released on Dec. 19, it was clear why there was such an intense argument. Nationally, the broadcast was CBS's second-highest rated regular-season game since the network began airing AFC games in 1998, and the highest since a 2007 Patriots-Colts game.

In Denver, the numbers were even bigger. According to KCNC-Channel 4 news director Tim Weiland, the game received a 74 share – an astronomical number for a regular-season game. The Super Bowl, by comparison, drew a 78 share in Denver last February. (In 2010, when the Broncos were in the midst of their worst season in franchise history, the team was drawing a share in the low 40s.) Tebow and the Broncos did not beat Tom Brady and the Patriots. In fact, Tebow did not win again during the regular season, with ugly losses against Buffalo and Kansas City.

Come playoff time, fans were jumping off the bandwagon in droves. The average ticket price on Dec. 28, four days before the regular-season finale against the Chiefs: $409.69. Average ticket price before the playoff game against the Steelers: $272.54.

Against Pittsburgh, however, Tebow was at his best. After a slow start, he threw for 316 yards, including the game-winning 80-yard pass to Demaryius Thomas on the first play of overtime for a 29-23 upset victory. He threw two touchdown passes and had a passer rating of 125.6. He also ran 10 times for 50 yards and a score.

After lackluster performances against Buffalo and Kansas City, it was all Tebow's critics could do to not say, "Told ya so."

With the stunning playoff victory, Tebowmania bypassed neutral as it shifted from reverse to overdrive.

More than 44 million people tuned in to watch Tebow and the Broncos beat the Steelers. In subsequent days, ESPN's "SportsCenter" devoted the bulk of its early portion of the show to Tebow reports. USA Today ran two Tebow centerpiece stories the next week – on page 1A.

Tebowmania never did die. It simply went into a two-week hibernation. And it awoke with a roar.

EVERYBODY WAS PUMPED FOR THE PATRIOTS GAME, INCLUDING COMPETING NETWORKS. *John Leyba, The Denver Post*

WHILE ELWAY CATCHES WRATH OF FANS, TEBOW, BRONCOS GO ON A WINNING STREAK

After Tim Tebow broke containment from the pocket and rumbled 20 yards for a touchdown with 58 seconds remaining to give the Broncos still another exhilarating win, this time 17-13 against the bombastic Rex Ryan and the New York Jets, the headline in the Denver Post the next day read:

In the nick of Tim

It was the type of headline that might have prompted New York Post copy editors to say: Why didn't we think of that?

All was going well in Tebow's World. He had led the Broncos to three victories in a row and was 4-1 in five starts. Three of those four victories came on second-half comebacks.

Sure, coach Fox had said in the days prior to the Jets game that if Tebow had to run a conventional offense, "he'd be screwed." But Tebow wasn't running a conventional offense. And he was winning. So Fox's comment, while provocative, had become irrelevant. Besides, Fox apologized. He said he was wrong for saying what he did.

All was forgiven after the Jets win. The Broncos were suddenly in the hunt for the AFC West title. At 5-5, they were alone in second place, one game behind the 6-4 Oakland Raiders.

Because the game against the Jets was played on a Thursday night, the Broncos were off from Friday afternoon through Sunday night. Life was good.

EVEN WITH TEBOW'S SUCCESS ON THE FIELD, BRIAN XANDERS AND JOHN ELWAY WERE OUT SCOUTING. *Craig F. Walker, The Denver Post*

Two days later, though, on Saturday, Nov. 19, guess who was scouting the Oklahoma-Baylor game in Waco, Texas? None other than John Elway and Brian Xanders, the top two ranking executives in the Broncos' front office.

Guess who the biggest stars were for the Oklahoma Sooners and Baylor Bears? For OU, quarterback Landry Jones, and for Baylor, eventual Heisman Trophy winner Robert Griffin III.

The Broncos' brass came away impressed with both quarterbacks. When the scouting trip was scheduled, the Broncos were 4-5. And if, heaven forbid, they finished 4-12? The Broncos would be looking for a quarterback in the draft.

Fans don't understand that teams don't make plans based on best-case scenarios. Yes, sports executives and coaches are optimists by nature. But whether you are running a Fortune 500 company, a small business or a football team, it's imperative that you not get caught ill-prepared. By its very nature, proper planning requires preparing for the worst. And so Elway and Xanders scouted Jones and Griffin.

Not because they didn't believe in Tebow. Because their jobs demanded it.

Then came Elway's radio show on the following Monday morning. With one stream-of-consciousness comment - that he didn't know if Tebow was the team's quarterback of the future - Elway had inadvertently created another Tebow disturbance that sent ripples through the national media.

Tebow was 4-1. Never mind that some of his throws wobbled worse than Gwyneth Paltrow in the movie "Country Strong."

Elway then explained that Tebow needed to improve his throwing on third down.

But all that was picked up on blogs across the country was: "Um, no."

Denver Post columnist Dave Krieger wrote:

Twitter has become known for many things during its short life, but civility is not one of them. So when John Elway chose the massively popular microblogging service as his method of direct communication with Broncos fans, he was taking a calculated risk.

The Broncos' transparency offensive was working pretty well, too, until Elway got crosswise with Tebowmania. Then it got ugly pretty fast.

"You know, I've actually stopped reading it, which is a good thing," Elway said with a laugh during his weekly hit on KOA radio Wednesday.

Here's a sampling of Twitter messages sent his way after he said earlier this week he didn't know if Tim Tebow was the Broncos' quarterback of the future:

"@johnelway i hope pat fires you and you can go back to arena football were (sic) you belong you piece of trash."

"@johnelway You are so damn clueless!"

"Hey@johnelway you lost 3 superbowls and your team won 2 for you when u were washed up so shut your (expletive) mouth"

"How does it feel@johnelway from being our hero to be almost as hated as Philip Rivers."

And so on. (The more vile comments were left out of a family newspaper.) When Tony Dungy, a former player and coach and more recently a Christian author, says of the Broncos, as he did the other day, "They're going to have to get some more passing game someway," most NFL heads nod in agreement.

When Elway says approximately the same thing, Denver has a conniption.

Trying to have a rational public conversation about Tebow is mostly futile these days. The subject has passed into a realm normally occupied by politics and religion, where people already know what they think and once the usual talking points are exhausted, the argument often devolves into personal insults.

Because Elway shares the doubts of many league insiders about long-term success without a robust passing game, and because he's forthright enough to say so, he is now routinely accused of being jealous of Tebow's popularity and wanting him to fail.

• • •

Elway later admitted he fumbled the interview, saying, "I was too blunt."

He subsequently tried to communicate his support of Tebow, often stating he's "very hopeful that Tim Tebow is our guy." He would tell Arnie Stapleton of The Associated Press that under no uncertain terms Tebow would be back with the Broncos next year.

Through it all, Elway tried to go as far as possible in supporting Tebow while also not issuing guarantees.

Tebow, meanwhile, kept stringing together wins. The Chargers, remember, were still considered the team to beat in the AFC West. They may have been struggling, losing five in a row. But they still had the division's best quarterback in Philip Rivers, and in Game 11 for both teams, the Chargers would play a home game against the Broncos.

Following the game, a 16-13 overtime Broncos win that featured another late Tebow comeback, The Denver Post's irrepressible columnist Woody Paige wrote:

SAN DIEGO » TeboWWWWW!

The Broncos got their fifth "W" - four wins in a row, two in overtime, three on fourth-quarter comebacks, every one dramatic in the second half - since Tim Tebow became

TEBOW FANS TOOK TO SIGNAGE AND TO TWITTER TO QUESTION AND CRITICIZE JOHN ELWAY. *John Leyba, The Denver Post*

quarterback.

And what about that McGahEEEEE, MilleRRRRR, DeckeRRRRR, EdEEEEE, PrateRRRRR, BailEEEEE, CladEEEEE and their partners dancing the Foxtrot!

In the locker room after their 16-13 victory over the Chargers on Sunday, the Broncos were screaming like teenage girls at a Justin Bieber concert.

The Broncos' tour de force (three consecutive victories in AFC West opponents' stadiums, four straight victories on the road) has become bigger and better than Bieber.

Who among us would have believed the Broncos could be 6-5 after a 1-4 start? They're in the playoff group photo. Oh, we of little faith.

"It's chicken and egg," John Fox said. "Winning builds confidence in the players that they can win."

• • •

As usual, Paige was having fun with the Tebow run.

Wrote The Denver Post's Mike Klis of the same game:

SAN DIEGO » This was why the Broncos drafted Tim Tebow in the first round. It was for this game, against this opponent, to outplay, if not necessarily outpass, the Broncos' primary nemesis, Philip Rivers.

If the Broncos were going to win the Super Bowl for the first time since the 1998 season, they would first have to win the AFC West.

For the better part of the past seven years, the Chargers were considered the division's team to beat. For going on the past six seasons, Rivers was considered the best quarterback in the division.

In a remarkably hard-fought, muscle-wearing rival matchup that took nearly a full extra quarter to decide, Tebow and the Broncos beat Rivers

WILL TO WIN: CHAPTER 10

JOSH McDANIELS SAW SOMETHING IN TEBOW THAT HE LIKED, TRADING PICKS TO TAKE THE RUN-ORIENTED QUARTERBACK WITH THE 25TH PICK IN THE DRAFT. IT WAS AN ODD FIT, TEBOW'S STYLE WITH McDANIELS' PREFERENCE FOR A POCKET PASSER.
Joe Amon, The Denver Post

and the Chargers 16-13 in overtime on a warm Sunday afternoon at Qualcomm Stadium.

Any chance Broncos fans can start to realize not everything about the abbreviated Josh McDaniels era in Denver was bad?

"I'm happy we have him," coach John Fox said of Tebow.

As the Broncos' first-year coach, Fox is the beneficiary of McDaniels' controversial choice with the No. 25 pick in the 2010 draft.

Against the Chargers, Tebow accounted for 210 total yards with 143 yards passing and 67 yards rushing – on a whopping 22 carries, many off the much-discussed read option that Fox implemented four games – and four wins – ago. Rivers accounted for 189 total yards with 188 yards passing and 1 yard rushing.

Just like the Broncos drew it up.

"He's a great quarterback," Tebow said of Rivers. "And a great guy. We have the same agent, so we've gotten to know each other pretty well."

It was McDaniels who thought Tebow could give the Broncos a counter to Rivers in the annual twice-a-year meetings for AFC West supremacy. It wasn't just that Rivers has always been an elite quarterback. What also struck McDaniels about Rivers is his fiery competitiveness.

The Broncos needed to counter that uber-competitiveness. As Tebow rallied the Broncos to victory despite deficits of 15-0 with three minutes remaining at Miami two months ago, 24-14 midway through the third quarter at Oakland, 13-10 inside the two-minute warning against the New York Jets and 13-10 again Sunday with less than two minutes remaining in regulation against the Chargers, is there any question about Tebow's competitiveness?

Said Brian Xanders, the Denver general manager who worked alongside McDaniels during the 2010 draft: "We looked at him as, had a great winning record at Florida. He had competitive toughness. High-end production in the running game and passing game in college. We knew he had to improve in the passing game, but he had a lot of traits we were looking for."

Tebow doesn't get it done by conventional NFL quarterback methods. But he gets it done. The Broncos have won five of the six games he has started this year and are 6-5, in position to reach the AFC playoffs for the first time since 2005. The Broncos trail the 7-4 Oakland Raiders by one game in the AFC West and the 7-4 Cincinnati Bengals by one game for an AFC wild card. ... Afterward, a shiner on his right cheek, Tebow was collecting his postgame meal near the buses when Rivers walked by. "Good job, Tim," he said.

• • •

Next came the 35-32, second-half shootout win at Minnesota. It was five wins in a row. Better yet for the Broncos, their 7-5 overall record moved them into a first-place tie in the AFC West with the Raiders, who got drilled at Miami 34-14 on the same day.

Broncos media relations boss Patrick Smyth already had it figured

> "We knew he had to improve in the passing game, **but he had a lot of traits we were looking for."**
>
> **Brian Xanders,** Broncos general manager

112   THE DENVER POST

XANDERS AND MCDANIELS LIKED TEBOW'S TOUGHNESS, A WILLINGNESS TO DO WHATEVER IT TOOK TO WIN. *John Leyba, The Denver Post*

WILL TO WIN: CHAPTER 10

out that Denver would own the tiebreakers if they came into play at season's end.

Tebow and the Broncos were advancing past fun and looking at gaining their first playoff appearance since 2005.

Next up: the Chicago Bears – with no Jay Cutler.

• • •

When the 2011 Broncos schedule first came out, the Bears game figured to be the marquee matchup of the season: Jay Cutler vs. Kyle Orton, who were traded for each other in 2009. Or maybe Jay Cutler vs. Tim Tebow.

Either way, Cutler, the Broncos' franchise quarterback when he was drafted with the No. 11 overall pick in 2006, would play the villain for his part in forcing a trade out of town following the 2008 season.

But Cutler would return to Denver only in a sweat suit. He tore up his thumb a couple of weeks earlier while trying to make a tackle on an interception return. His replacement was Caleb Hanie, a former Colorado State quarterback who struggled mightily in his first real opportunity to play at the NFL level.

Hanie had thrown six interceptions in his first two games, both losses, since Cutler's injury.

Leading into the Bears-Broncos game, though, the story wasn't Cutler or Hanie. The story wasn't even Tebow and his five-game winning streak. At least not directly.

The story was the battle between CBS and NBC over the rights to the following week's game between the Patriots and Broncos, matching New England's esteemed quarterback, Tom Brady, against Denver's transcendent one. It took three days of intense squabbling before NFL commissioner Roger Goodell stepped in and awarded the game to CBS.

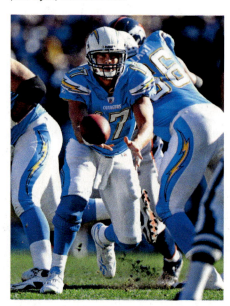

PHILIP RIVERS AND TEBOW SHARED AN AGENT AND A FIERY COMPETITIVE NATURE. RIVERS WOULD COME THROUGH FOR THE BRONCOS ON THE LAST DAY OF THE REGULAR SEASON.

John Leyba, The Denver Post

Even The Denver Post editorial page couldn't resist weighing in. Wrote The Post on its op-ed page:

NBC's failed bid to buy a last-minute ticket aboard the Tim Tebow Train is the latest of numerous signals that the locomotive is picking up speed – not just in Broncos Country, but across the entire country.

Tebow is the face of what had been a moribund franchise that finds itself back in the spotlight following wins in six of his seven starts at quarterback. (Dare we offer up a thank you to Josh McDaniels?) His faith-first, run-second and win-at-every-turn style at the game's glamour position makes him one of its most popular, yet polarizing figures.

While Tebow's willingness to profess his faith in Jesus Christ grates on some, we don't fault him for sharing his beliefs.

His habit of taking a knee in prayer on the sidelines has become a flattering/mocking fad dubbed Tebowing.

And Tebow remains unbowed. He starts many interviews by thanking his "Lord and savior, Jesus Christ." He frequently ends them with the words "God bless."

We can't remember a star athlete so openly and so regularly displaying his faith since Muhammad Ali.

What's remarkable about Tebow is that he remains humble even as his star soars to new levels.

This week, television executives went into overtime in a fight over "flexing" the Dec. 18 Denver-New England game from its afternoon time slot on CBS to prime time on NBC. The Sunday night broadcast is the flagship of the NFL television franchise, and it's fair to say there was something about the game pitting the first-place Patriots against the resurgent Broncos that was even more appealing for NBC: Tebow.

ESPN on Wednesday devoted nearly an entire hour of its "SportsCenter" franchise to the Broncos' unorthodox quarterback. Has that ever been done before?

Yet after leading the Broncos to another come-from-behind victory last week, Tebow told Sports Illustrated's Peter King what he was most proud of, which was being able to say the name of a young cancer patient in postgame interviews: "I let him know people cared about him. I let him know God has a plan for him."

Tebow's critics can cite numerous statistics to bolster their claims that his unconventional style isn't right for the NFL. Sometimes that criticism is a veil of intolerance for an athlete who wears his faith on his sleeve – or eye black, as the case may be. By the same token, Tebow supporters can be too quick to dismiss valid concerns or observations as heresy.

Does Tebow have room to grow as a quarterback? Absolutely. Will he lead a proud franchise back to the promised land? Time will tell. For now, he deserves a Mile High Salute

AS THE WINS PILED UP, SO DID THE MEDIA GLARE. NOT ALL PLAYERS AROUND THE LEAGUE LIKED IT. *Joe Amon, The Denver Post*

not just for helping the Broncos string together a series of wins, but refusing to run from his evangelical Christian beliefs.

While some would begrudge him, we think the way in which Tebow carries himself is something everyone, regardless of faith, can learn a lesson from.

• • •

So this is what the people outside the newsroom's toy department thought. Rarely do the nerds bother forming an opinion on something as trivial as football. Tebow, though, was a crossover rarity.

The winning streak reached six when the Broncos again pulled out an improbable 13-10 win over the Bears in overtime.

Improbable? In Tebow's first win, he led the Broncos back from a 15-0 deficit at Miami with less than three minutes remaining. In what turned out to be Tebow's last regular-season win, the Broncos were trailing the Bears 10-0 with under three minutes remaining.

It got to the point where The Post felt compelled to rank Tebow's six – count 'em, six – second-half comeback wins, five of which came in the fourth quarter. A quick poll of Broncos coaches and players revealed the Miami win was No. 1. The Bears win was a close second.

Wrote Mike Klis in the Dec. 13 edition:

Even if a 10-0 deficit isn't as insurmountable as 15-0, it's still two scores. And the Broncos didn't start their comeback until they got the ball with 4:34 remaining in this game, or 49 fewer seconds than when they began their comeback in Miami.

Another problem for the Broncos in their attempted comeback was, unlike in their Miami win, they failed to recover a recoverable onside kick with 2:08 remaining.

Like Miami, Tebow showed few signs during most of the game that a comeback was in him. He was 3-of-

> "We have a guy here that's breaking records every week, and you have a guy in Tebow that's saying 'God' every word **and he gets coverage.**"
>
> Green Bay tight end **Jermichael Finley**

16 passing for 45 yards after three quarters, although there were five dropped passes. In the fourth quarter and overtime, though, Tebow was 18-of-24 for 191 yards and a touchdown, for a 111.6 passer rating.

After Tebow got the Broncos close with a TD pass to Thomas, he got Bears running back Marion Barber III to stop the clock by running out of bounds, he got Barber to fumble in overtime, and he got field goals of 59 yards by Prater to tie it at the end of regulation and 51 yards in overtime to win it.

• • •

The Raiders, meanwhile, were trounced again, this time 46-16 at Green Bay. The Broncos were 8-5 and alone in first place.

It had reached a point where people were beginning to wonder if Tebow had mystic powers. As the late comedian Johnny Carson might have said about how the breaks seemed to fall the Broncos' way late in games: "That is weird. Weird, weird stuff."

Looking back, the week between the Bears win and upcoming game against the great Tom Brady and the Patriots was the height of Tebowmania.

Smyth was getting up to 100 interview requests a week for Tebow. Smyth turned down both Jay Leno's night show and Matt Lauer's morning program. The NFL Network and ESPN sent reporters to Broncos headquarters not for the usual weekly feature, but for day-to-day updates. Newspapers and dot-comers descended upon Dove Valley to write Tebow features. For the second time in three weeks, Tebow was on the cover of Sports Illustrated.

It was Tebow, Tebow's style of play, Tebow's faith and the perception that Tebow had not completely sold Elway and Fox as a quarterback – however exaggerated these perceptions might have been – that made for a combustible cocktail of a story.

There was talk not only about Tebow making the AFC Pro Bowl team despite not playing in the first 4½ games of the season, but as a strong runner-up MVP candidate to Green Bay quarterback Aaron Rodgers.

Rodgers' Packers were 13-0 but overshadowed by the Broncos, the league's hottest story. Tebow was even hotter.

And now it wasn't just the former player/current NFL analyst who was resentful. Tebow's success, and the enormous publicity of that success, was bringing a backlash from current players.

Carolina Panthers star receiver Steve Smith said when it comes to comparing rookie Cam Newton to Tim Tebow, his teammate was by far the better NFL quarterback.

"If Tebow is standing next to me, I would tell it to his face – come check me out in five years, Jack, and you'll know who's the best quarterback," Smith said in a story circulated by The AP. "You can't compare Cam to Tebow. I think Cam's a more complete player."

As so often happens in athletic locker rooms, once a guy dares to say something, others pile on.

Baltimore Ravens quarterback Joe Flacco, whose comments are usually double-dipped in vanilla, was on a local radio show when he started complaining about how Tebow was hogging the spotlight from everyone, including his team.

"I don't want to see Tim do bad, but look what happens after he wins a football game," Flacco said. "If you watched SportsCenter (Monday) it was Tim Tebow, then something else. Tim Tebow, then something else. And Tim Tebow, then something else.

"When we beat the Steelers, were we on TV? No. I couldn't even find a Baltimore Ravens highlight."

Good thing Flacco made it clear he didn't want to see Tebow do bad.

In Green Bay, tight end Jermichael Finley stuck up for his guy Rodgers by calling the attention on Tebow "kind of disturbing."

"We have a guy here that's breaking records every week, and you have a guy in Tebow that's saying 'God' every word and he gets coverage," Finley told the Milwaukee Journal Sentinel. "Of course, I love my faith and God, but come on, man!

"He's telling everybody what they want to hear. You see him and he's patting everybody on the back saying, 'You're going to make this catch. I promise because God said,' and he makes it happen. Stuff like that. It confuses people.

"People that don't know the game outside of the fans, of course, they're going to hype it up. But guys that

ANOTHER IMPROBABLE COMEBACK SET UP A HIGHLY ANTICIPATED MEETING WITH THE PATRIOTS. *Joe Amon, The Denver Post*

see a good player and a good quarterback, they know what kind of guy he'll be down the road when he gets exposed. Everybody who knows the game knows what kind of player Tebow is going to be."

Finley pretty much said Tebow stinks as a player and is popular only because of his faith. What Smith, Flacco and Finley failed to point out in their criticisms is Tebow asked for none of the attention he received.

Yet, only with Tebow do current players break the unwritten code of bashing a fellow player.

Patriots coach Bill Belichick, of course, had nothing but kind words for Tebow during the week leading up to the Dec. 18 game. Brady, interestingly enough, deflected questions he received about Tebow during the week by continually praising the Broncos as a whole and saying little about his opposing quarterback.

After a week of hype similar to the days leading up to Super Bowl XXXIII to cap the 1998 season, which everyone figured would be Elway's final game as Broncos quarterback, it was time to play the Patriots.

It would become a time when critics of Tebow would start loading up evidence in support of their argument.

THE DENVER POST 117

WILL TO WIN: CHAPTER 11

MOMENTUM SWINGS AGAINST THE BRONCOS AS DEFENSES FIGURE OUT TEBOW

Brady Quinn, the backup quarterback to Tim Tebow, was in a casual conversation with a Denver Post reporter about how the Broncos had been so hot, and then suddenly they were not.

It happens all the time to major-league baseball teams during a 162-game season. A team will go on a winning streak, and as soon as they lose one game, more losses often start piling up.

Same team, same players, same coaches, same talent, same decisions. Not necessarily the same breaks, though. And not the same results.

"You know about quantum physics as it relates to momentum?" Quinn asked.

While he was a star quarterback at Notre Dame, Quinn took a physics class. Not only took it, he enjoyed it. That physics class stayed with him five years out of college. This past summer, he rented a house in the Denver area, and one of his neighbors was Steve Olsen, a professor in quantum physics.

Olsen and Quinn started talking. Olsen would teach. Quinn would listen.

"He explained how momentum swings in a game is actually tied to quantum physics," Quinn said. "I started researching quantum physics and how one's beliefs can have an instrumental effect on the outcome of any situation."

And to think fans stereotype football players as dummies.

Quinn is no mad scientist. Included in the definition of quantum physics is this: Electric and magnetic fields possess momentum regardless of whether they are static or they change in time.

THE BRONCOS GOT BEAT BY A BILLS TEAM THAT ENTERED THE GAME WITH A SEVEN-GAME LOSING STREAK. *Hyoung Chang, The Denver Post*

WILL TO WIN: CHAPTER 11

TEBOW AND THE BRONCOS CAME OUT FIRED UP FOR THE PATRIOTS AT MILE HIGH. THEIR OFFENSE WAS CLICKING, TOO, SCORING TOUCHDOWNS ON THEIR FIRST TWO POSSESSIONS. ONLY TROUBLE WAS THAT NEW ENGLAND QUARTERBACK TOM BRADY WAS HAVING HIS WAY WITH THE BRONCOS' DEFENSE. *Steve Nehf, The Denver Post*

Momentum, then, is as much physical as it is mystical. Just because momentum has its physical elements, though, doesn't mean it can be bottled.

The same Broncos team that played so wondrously during its six-game winning streak was suddenly getting bullied by the weakest of the NFL's weak during the tail end of a three-game losing streak. Like all momentum shifts, though, there were warning signs.

Overshadowed in those near-miraculous victories was the fact that opponents were getting a better idea of how to stop Tebow and the Broncos' read-option offense.

The first team to crack the option code was the San Diego Chargers, who were Game 4 in the streak. Tebow carried the ball a quarterback-record 22 times – 22 rushes by a quarterback!? – but for only 67 yards, a 3.0-yard average. His longest run was 12 yards.

The Chargers, it seems, used a less-is-more approach.

"To keep him under control, we were slowing down our rushes," defensive lineman Tommie Harris said.

The following week, the Minnesota Vikings' defense held Tebow and the Broncos' offense to one first down in the first half. That's right – one first down by halftime.

Forgotten amid Tebow's sensational second half, in which he completed 6-of-8 passes for a whopping 178 yards – 29.6 yards per completion – was the Broncos' abandonment of read-option plays. Tebow lit up the Vikings and their porous secondary for 28 second-half points, but all but ignored was his meager 13 yards rushing on four carries.

Defenses were getting a blueprint on how to stop Tebow. They just couldn't come up with a way to counterspell Tebow's magic.

The Bears? Again, Tebow and the Broncos were shut out with fewer than three minutes left.

The Broncos were finding ways to win with late-game magic, but defenses were starting to solve the Tebow riddle.

As Harris indicated, the defensive ends in a 4-3 defense, or outside linebackers in a 3-4, were not rushing from the edge anymore. The defenses were bringing pressure up the middle, either by allowing the defensive tackles to penetrate instead of holding their ground, or stunting a linebacker up the middle, or both.

With pressure up the middle, Tebow would try to escape to the outside of the pocket – where the non-rushing defensive ends or outside linebackers were waiting for him. It was like a slow leak through a small hole in a dam wall. After rallying to defeat the Bears in overtime for win No. 6 in the six-game winning streak, the first seismic momentum shift occurred during the New England game Dec. 18, then continued to roll full steam through the final two weeks of the regular season.

After incredible hype leading into the New England game, the Broncos came out emotionally and mentally charged on an unseasonably warm afternoon at Sports Authority Field at Mile High. The Broncos took the opening kickoff and easily moved 80 yards for a touchdown.

Tebow and tailback Willis McGahee took turns running effectively through New England's front seven. Tebow finished off the drive with a 9-yard touchdown run.

On their second possession, the Broncos needed only four plays to move 82 yards. McGahee rambled for 29 yards. Tebow hit Demaryius Thomas for 22, and Lance Ball sprinted down the right side for a 32-

TEAMS WERE FIGURING TEBOW OUT. THE CHARGERS' DEFENSE LIMITED HIM TO 67 YARDS IN 22 CARRIES. *Joe Amon, The Denver Post*

yard touchdown. The only problem with the drive was McGahee strained his hamstring on his long run.

Third drive, again the Broncos moved the ball with ease. Tebow hit Eric Decker for 22 yards, and the quarterback later ran off right guard for 19.

The Broncos had first down in the red zone, but this time the drive stalled. Still, the Broncos had two touchdowns and a field goal after three possessions.

Problem was, New England quarterback Tom Brady was slicing up the Broncos' defense. Despite their early offensive success, the Broncos were ahead only 16-14 when they got the ball for their fourth possession.

And then quantum physics started to shift. Ball fumbled on the first play. The Pats turned the turnover into a short field goal and a 17-16 lead.

Next possession, third play, Tebow was caught in-between a decision whether to keep the ball or pitch it to Eddie Royal. Meanwhile, Pats' defensive lineman Mark Anderson whacked Tebow's arm. Fumble.

The Pats turned that mistake into a score – a 1-yard quarterback sneak by Brady.

As Mike Klis wrote in his game account for The Denver Post:

The quarterback got up after rushing for a touchdown and celebrated with great passion.

Take that, Tebowmania.

Is that what New England Patriots quarterback Tom Brady shouted as he ferociously spiked the ball in front of the north stands fans?

"Personally, that's what I took that as," Broncos cornerback André Goodman said. "Because of the buildup between Tebowmania vs. Brady, I think he took that personally. And football is a personal game. I

WILL TO WIN: CHAPTER 11

HAD BRADY TAKEN THE COMPETITION WITH TEBOW PERSONALLY? AFTER SCORING ON A 1-YARD RUN, HE SPIKED THE BALL INTO THE TURF. HE WENT ON TO COMPLETE 23-OF-34 PASSES FOR 320 YARDS, ACCOUNTING FOR TWO TOUCHDOWNS WITHOUT AN INTERCEPTION. *John Leyba, The Denver Post*

don't blame him for taking it personal. It was our job to keep him out of the end zone so he doesn't spike the ball."

• • •

It was 24-16 Patriots.

The next Broncos' possession was a three-and-out. Oh-oh. Momentum was clearly shifting from the Broncos.

With the first half ticking down to the final seconds, Broncos returner Quan Cosby tried to field a punt at his own 17. He dropped it and the Pats recovered, then kicked a field goal on the final play of the half.

It was 27-16 Patriots. And just like that, a Broncos team that had won six in a row, and was leading 16-7, had lost its mojo.

The most encouraging aspect of the game for the Broncos was Tebow completing passes he hadn't hit all season. Still, the Patriots cruised to a 41-23 win. No one expected the Broncos to win them all. Still, the hype and emotion that stirred the Broncos entering the game seemingly left them crashed like a coffee-addict at 2 p.m.

The Denver Post game story read:

In many ways, Tebow had the best passing game of his career. Maybe not statistically, but this was a game where he looked like a passer. He threw in rhythm. He was accurate on midrange slants and sideline patterns. He completed 11-of-22 for 194 yards and also gained 93 yards rushing on 12 carries.

He led his offense to touchdowns on his first two possessions and another in the fourth quarter, when in previous weeks he has been magical.

"I thought he improved," Broncos coach John Fox said.

Tebow entered the game with a 7-1 record and a six-game winning streak. Brady entered as one of the best and winningest quarterbacks in NFL history. He has three Super Bowl rings and a 16-0 regular season to his credit.

Picking apart a Broncos secondary filled with rookies, Brady completed 23-of-34 for 320 yards, two touchdowns and zero interceptions. And, yes, he had a 1-yard rushing touchdown, followed by a menacing spike, in the second quarter that put the Pats up 24-16 after they had once trailed 16-7.

The Broncos fell to 8-6 but still lead the AFC West by one game with two remaining. They can clinch the division in one of two ways: Win next week at Buffalo and second-place Oakland loses at Kansas City; or, even if the Broncos lose at Buffalo next week, they would clinch the playoffs by defeating Kyle Orton and the Kansas City Chiefs in the season finale Jan. 1.

The first playoff appearance in six years still is there for the Broncos, but competing against an elite team like the Patriots, who have been NFL royalty since 2001 and just clinched another AFC East title with an 11-3 record?

Not yet. All was going well for the Broncos until they started treating the ball like it contained a deadly infectious disease.

• • •

The Broncos were still leading the AFC West because the Raiders blew a 27-14, fourth-quarter lead at Detroit and lost 28-27.

"We're all right," Tebow said. "We're excited about where we're at, and we're going to continue to be positive and stay motivated and just try to improve."

Tebow was only half-correct. The Broncos were all right, as it turned out. Looking back, they had essentially clinched their division when they came back to beat the Bears.

But the immediate future would bring regression, not improvement, and far more negatives than positives.

Six days after they fell apart at home against New England, the

FIRST-HALF TURNOVERS HELPED NEW ENGLAND CUT INTO AND THEN ERASE AN EARLY BRONCOS' LEAD. *Tim Rasmussen, The Denver Post*

WILL TO WIN: CHAPTER 11

XANDERS, ELWAY AND FOX HAD WAIVED KYLE ORTON ONLY TO SEE HIM RETURN TO MILE HIGH WITH THE CHIEFS AND BEAT THE BRONCOS ON THE FINAL GAME OF THE REGULAR SEASON IN WHAT WAS TEBOW'S WORST GAME AS A PRO. *Steve Nehf, The Denver Post*

Broncos spent Christmas Eve in Buffalo. They got embarrassed 40-14 by a Bills team that entered the game with a seven-game losing streak.

This was when political satirist Bill Maher sent out his profane tweet that mocked the trinity of Tebow, Jesus and Christmas.

No doubt Tebow was an easy target. He threw three interceptions and fumbled once, with two of the mistakes returned for touchdowns. Tebow had played the worst game of his life. NFL, college, high school, Pop Warner, whatever. His worst game ever.

Against the Bills, of all teams.

"Coming into this game, we knew that to give us a better chance of winning, we had to make them one-dimensional," Bills safety George Wilson said. "We had to do that by winning on first and second down. That would put them in third-and-long situations and force Tebow to throw. When he was in that situation, we were able to get pressure on him with our front seven and forced some errant throws."

It was hardly consolation that a week later, Tebow's performance against the Bills dropped to the second-worst game of his career.

No doubt, quantum physics had deviously turned on the Broncos when the team was left to play none other than Kyle Orton with nothing less than the playoffs at stake.

The Broncos did not want it to work out this way. When they released Orton on Nov. 22, they made a calculated gamble. They could save the remaining $2.6 million on his contract if another team claimed him.

Three teams did. Check.

They could free up the awkwardness in the locker room and allow Tebow to become himself. Check.

But how embarrassing would it be for the Broncos' decision-making triumvirate of Elway-Fox-Xanders if their decision to release Orton came back to cost them a shot at the playoffs? Orton wound up with the Chiefs, whom the Broncos would play in the final game of the regular season in Denver. The Broncos were hoping they could clinch the division title against Buffalo, which would render the final game against Orton meaningless. No check here.

Wrote Lindsay H. Jones for Denver Post readers on the morning of the Jan. 1 game:

Never in the 41-year history of the modern NFL, since the merger with the AFL, has a quarterback returned to start a game in the same season against his former team. And perhaps never have two head coaches worked so hard during the week to quiet talk of a quarterback duel, emphasizing that today's game is team vs. team, not quarterback vs. quarterback.

"I think it's proved to be a good decision," Broncos coach John Fox said of going with Tebow over Orton. "Anytime you make a decision, there's a lot of things that go into it. Without getting into all the particulars, I thought it was, all in all, best for everybody."

It wasn't an easy decision, nor one made without careful consideration of the risks involved should Orton wind up with an upcoming opponent.

The Broncos say they got what they wanted, however. Financially, they were able to pass the $2.6 million remaining on Orton's contract to Kansas City, which was awarded Orton off waivers ahead of Dallas and Chicago, both also having put in a claim for the veteran QB. In the Denver locker room, Orton's departure solidified the message that Tebow was in charge.

"Tim always had the capability, but with the air cleared, he was able to be himself and express himself and not feel like he has to put himself into a shell," said wide receiver Eric Decker.

The Chiefs, meanwhile, acquired a quarterback who was a significant

124 THE DENVER POST

TAKING THE CHARGERS' CUE, THE VIKINGS' DEFENSE HELD THE BRONCOS TO ONE FIRST DOWN IN THE FIRST HALF. *John Leyba, The Denver Post*

upgrade over the inexperienced Tyler Palko, who was 0-4 after replacing the injured Matt Cassel. In his first start two weeks ago, Orton helped the Chiefs beat previously undefeated Green Bay. An overtime loss at home last weekend to Oakland, however, knocked Kansas City out of playoff contention.

The uncertain part of the decision will be answered today. A loss by the Broncos (8-7) today wouldn't completely erase their playoff hopes. But their postseason chances then would depend on the Chargers beating the Raiders at Oakland in a game being played at the same time.

• • •

Against his former teammate – and nemesis – Tebow completed just 6-of-22 passes for 60 yards with a fumble and interception in a 7-3 loss.

That career-low 37.9 passer rating against Buffalo? He had a 20.6 rating against the Chiefs.

Just like that, the Broncos went from 8-5 and the most exciting story in football to 8-8 and reeling in a state of despondency.

The Broncos would get one more break. And it was a biggie: The Raiders lost their final game at home to San Diego. The Broncos, Raiders and Chargers all finished 8-8. The Chiefs finished 7-9.

The Broncos won the AFC West because they had a better record against common opponents than the Raiders and Chargers.

"A little bittersweet right now ...
But I think it's still a special thing what we accomplished, to come back to win the AFC West."

Tim Tebow, on losing to Kansas City in the final game of the regular season

Wrote Denver Post columnist Mark Kiszla:

Maybe this is the miracle of Tim Tebow: The Broncos win, even when they lose, lose, lose.

Any other NFL team that looked as inept as Denver did Sunday during a 7-3 loss to Kansas City would take a three-game losing streak and go home.

But The Tebow Show gets renewed for another week. It's good television, even when the quarterback plays bad football. That's the Tebow mystique.

"I don't know about any mystique. But I'm grateful for another opportunity," said Tebow after being outplayed by Orton.

Now for the tough questions:

Do the slumping Broncos have a prayer in the playoffs, which they will open at home against Pittsburgh?

"We keep putting that product out there like we did (today) and it's not going to be pretty," star cornerback Champ Bailey said.

• • •

The Broncos must have had just one more proton of quantum physics going for them in 2011 than they had in 2008. In 2008, the Broncos were 8-5 and leading the AFC West by three games with three to go. They lost all three, lost the division, and two days later, iconic coach Mike Shanahan was fired.

In 2011, the Broncos were 8-5, leading the AFC West by one game with three to go. They lost all three but won the division anyway.

Talk about your thin lines between success and failure.

Not that Tebow and Broncos coach John Fox were celebrating what they had just accomplished – the team's first playoff appearance in six years.

Wrote Mike Klis in his game story for The Denver Post:

This was a celebration without cheers. A party without music. Or food or drink. Or fun.

There is a team meeting at 9 a.m. today at Bronco headquarters. Maybe spirits will improve by then.

For the first time in six years, the Broncos are going to the playoffs as AFC West champions.

They won by losing. In a game the Broncos thought sure they had to win, they lost to former Broncos quarterback Kyle Orton and the Kansas City Chiefs 7-3 Sunday before a crowd of mixed feelings at Sports Authority Field at Mile High.

Yippee-ay-yawn.

The Broncos made the playoffs on the regular season's final day because their good friend Philip Rivers and the San Diego Chargers defeated the Oakland Raiders 38-26 on Sunday.

In the bigger scheme, the Broncos made the playoffs because of a six-game winning streak that stretched from Nov. 6 with a win at Oakland and ended Dec. 11 with an overtime win against the Chicago Bears.

Little did the Broncos know at the time they would need nothing more to win the AFC West. Just like in their head-to-head competitions during the past two training camps, Orton again beat Tebow.

Yet overall, Tebow was 7-4 as a starting quarterback and Orton was 1-4. Actually, in games started by Orton this year, the Broncos were 1-5.

It was Tebow who got the Broncos to the playoffs, even if he got them there three weeks before anyone realized.

"A little bittersweet right now," Tebow said. "We would have loved to have won that game and had a little bit more momentum going into the playoffs. But I think it's still a special thing what we accomplished, to come back to win the AFC West."

• • •

It hardly seemed special at the moment. It felt like the Broncos had backed into the playoffs by default. And the mighty Pittsburgh Steelers were next. The Steelers had been to three of the past six Super Bowls, winning two. They finished No. 1 in the league in scoring defense (14.2 points allowed), passing defense (171.9 yards per game) and total defense (271.8 yards per game).

Not exactly Tebow's idea of a Holy Trinity. The playoff drought was finally over, and what did the Broncos draw? The league's best defense at a time when their own quarterback was struggling mightily.

Although the Broncos would be playing at home, the Steelers would be an 8½-point favorite. After scoring just 14 points against the Bills and three points against the Chiefs, it was difficult to envision how the Broncos would score, let alone defeat, the Steelers.

BEATEN UP AFTER THE KANSAS CITY LOSS, TEBOW HAD TO WONDER WHAT OPPOSING DEFENSES HAD FIGURED OUT. *Steve Nehf, The Denver Post*

TEBOW WILL NEVER PLAY QUARTERBACK, RIGHT? THAT'S WHAT THEY KEEP SAYING

With the sun having long set beyond Sports Authority Field at Mile High and the temperature dropping below freezing on Jan. 8, 2012, four men gathered on the sideline to discuss a play call.

For once, Tim Tebow wasn't the most gung-ho person in the group. He was confident. Excited, even. But also calm, focused.

It was "Goose" who was the most enthusiastic about what had just happened. The Broncos had led 20-6 at halftime in their first playoff game since the 2005 season, but the heavily favored Pittsburgh Steelers had rallied behind Ben Roethlisberger, their superb, playoff-tested quarterback.

It was 23-23 at the end of regulation, and only a terrific play by defensive end Elvis Dumervil in the final seconds of regulation gave the fading Broncos one more chance in overtime. Dumervil poked the ball out of Big Ben's hands for a fumble and an 11-yard loss, backing the Steelers out of field-goal range. Tebow, who on his final pass of regulation had missed woefully low on a pass intended for a wide-open Demaryius Thomas cutting across midfield, would get another chance.

Immediately after Steelers captain James Farrior called "tails" and the overtime coin flip by referee Ron Winter came up "heads," Broncos offensive coordinator Mike McCoy, quarterbacks coach Adam "Goose" Gase, Thomas and Tebow huddled to discuss the first play call.

"All four of us got together and went over different looks, and I know Goose said it a few times: 'Hey, this could be it,' " Tebow said a couple of days later at

DEMARYIUS THOMAS GAVE IKE TAYLOR ONE SOLID STIFF-ARM, THEN HEADED FOR THE END ZONE. *AAron Ontiveroz, The Denver Post*

> "I know Goose said it a few times: 'Hey, this could be it.' I think he said it to Matt Willis: **'Remember, we score, we win.'**"
>
> Tim Tebow

his locker. "I think he said it to (wide receiver) Matt Willis: 'Remember, we score, we win.'"

The kickoff was a touchback, and Tebow ran out onto his home field with the ball at his own 20 for the first play of overtime. This moment was made for NFL's most analyzed contradiction.

Yes, Tebow was the quarterback who led the league in wounded spirals. But Tebow's six fourth-quarter comeback victories through 11 starts were far and away the most in NFL history.

"The first thought was the play fake," Tebow said. "We did a great job of selling it. Great fake by the backs. The Steelers were playing aggressive, so we had to give them a look like that quite a few times in the game. So we were able to get by the safety – he came up."

Thomas was split semi-wide left, covered by Steelers cornerback Ike Taylor. Steelers safety Ryan Mundy had been in deep protection on Thomas' side but edged up near the line of scrimmage as Tebow barked the cadence.

When Mundy moved up, the Steelers inexplicably had 11 men in the box. Not an eight-man box. They had 11 guys within a couple of yards of the line of scrimmage.

Talk about disrespecting Tebow as a passer.

Dick LeBeau, the Steelers' famed defensive coordinator, didn't know it at the time, but in a span of 11 seconds, he would pay for his arrogance.

Tebow faked a read-option handoff to running back Willis McGahee. That fake caused the Steelers' other safety, Troy Polamalu, who had been playing up in linebacker's row on the opposite side of Thomas and Taylor, to hesitate for a second.

Thomas got off the line clean, then cut toward the middle of the field at a diagonal into the area Mundy had just vacated. Tebow zipped his pass with authority. Thomas caught it with two hands, helmet-high, at the 38-yard line – meaning Tebow, the quarterback who supposedly did not have the arm strength or accuracy to play at the NFL level, had hummed the ball 25 yards on a rope to hit Thomas in stride.

"Watching it on film, the linebackers did a great job of playing it," Tebow said. "They were able to roll up and get their hands up, but we were able to get the second window behind them. Behind the linebackers. And D.T. did a good job of flattening it off coming across. The corner kind of went high, so he flattened it off a little more so I was to lead him across. He caught it. And made the rest happen."

Mundy scrambled in retreat as Taylor chased Thomas down at the 45. But just as Taylor closed, Thomas kept him at bay with a knee-buckling stiff-arm. Taylor never recovered.

Polamalu, the all-pro safety, had first looked in at McGahee, then veered toward Eddie Royal, the Broncos' second receiver on the play who ran a button-hook on the other side of the field. Although Royal was running essentially a decoy route, he carried it out with such force that he attracted three defenders.

The play call, formation and execution had completely removed the great Polamalu from the play.

Mundy, subbing for Ryan Clark, the Steelers' starting safety who was unable to play because of a medical condition that leaves him vulnerable at altitude, recovered enough to seemingly have the angle on Thomas. But Thomas outran the angle, sprinting to and through the end zone, and into the tunnel that led to what was now the victorious home locker room.

Touchdown. Broncos win. The Broncos had just beaten the Steelers 29-23 in a wild-card playoff game.

Wrote Mike Klis in his game story for The Denver Post:

The sellout crowd of more than 75,000 at Sports Authority Field at Mile High erupted. Witnesses said that in Denver neighborhoods, delirious people were screaming from their balconies. Patrons at Denver-area bars were heard chanting, "Te-bow! Te-bow!"

Tebowmania is once again inflated.

• • •

Tebow had done it again, coming through when the pressure was greatest. Tebow had led the Broncos to eight wins in the 2011 season, seven of those by seven points or fewer.

Yet there were times when respect from his peers remained elusive.

"He's a good running back, man," said Bears linebacker Brian Urlacher, when asked about Tebow after the Broncos rallied from 10-0 down with less than three minutes remaining to win 13-10 in overtime.

AFTER THE WIN OVER THE STEELERS, TEBOW COULD LOOK FORWARD TO A REMATCH WITH THE PATRIOTS. Hyoung Chang, The Denver Post

Tebow, taking over one of the worst teams in the league, led the Broncos to a 7-4 record in their final 11 regular-season games, good enough to reach the playoffs as AFC West Division champs. Still, by season's end, Tebow's critics were multiplying in number and becoming harsher in their analysis.

That 7-4 mark, after all, had been 7-1 until the Broncos finished the season with three consecutive losses. Tebow played poorly in the last two. In fact, they were the worst two games of his life, losses to Buffalo and Kansas City.

And, no doubt, the Broncos were fortunate to be playing in the mild, mild AFC West, where they held tiebreakers against Oakland and San Diego, who also finished 8-8.

Yet, for all the knocks he received, Tebow also may have been the NFL player who was showered with the most love. Maybe ever. Before he had a chance to put on his No. 15 Broncos jersey, it was No. 1 in NFL sales. He had inspired a globalized "Tebowing" craze. There is a long list of churches across the country offering hefty fees in hopes the Broncos' quarterback and arguably America's most influential Christian will speak to their congregation. He once had the networks fighting three days for the rights to telecast his game, a

| | | | WILL TO WIN: CHAPTER 12 | | | |

THERE WASN'T MUCH TO SAY, TRAILING THE PATRIOTS BADLY IN THE FOURTH QUARTER. OFFENSIVE COORDINATOR MIKE McCOY (RIGHT), TEBOW AND QUARTERBACKS COACH ADAM GASE HAD HAD BETTER DAYS. *John Leyba, The Denver Post*

By upsetting the Steelers, the Broncos earned the right to play the No. 1-seeded Patriots in a second-round AFC playoff game, a rematch from a month earlier that this time would be played in Foxborough, Mass. The wise guys in Vegas still didn't think much of the Broncos; the Patriots were whopping 13½-point favorites.

Starting with coach John Fox's decision to defer after winning the opening coin toss, New England was in an attack mode. A proud veteran team, the Patriots had earned a No. 1 playoff seed and accompanying bye week, which meant they got an extra week to clear their minds, steel their resolve and freshen their legs. And the frigid New England night air seemed to have teeth biting through skin. Tom Brady had performed through the frigid elements before. Tebow was about to play in the coldest game of his life.

A limping prairie rodent beneath a sky of circling hawks might have gotten better odds.

For all the hype given to Tebow and Brady in the days leading up to the game, the biggest issue for the Broncos was they didn't have anybody who could cover a quality tight end. And the Patriots have arguably the best 1-2 tight end combination in NFL history.

Wrote Mike Klis in his setup for the Jan. 14 game:

Broncos cornerback Champ Bailey, good as he is, can't cover New England Patriots tight end Rob Gronkowski.

At 6-foot-6, 265 pounds, Gronkowski is too big.

André Goodman, one of the league's more solid No. 2 corners, is not who the Broncos want defending the Patriots' Wes Welker, who is the NFL's top slot receiver. The 5-foot-9 Welker is too quick.

Then there's New England tight

dispute eventually settled by commissioner Roger Goodell.

Elway, the greatest player in Broncos history, thought his own fishbowl existence as a young, franchise quarterback in the 1980s was difficult.

"I don't think what I went through compared to what Tim went through this year," Elway said. "What I went through was more locally based. When you look at Tim Tebow, what he went through was nationally based, or maybe even worldwide based. When you talk about people Tebowing by the Eiffel Tower, that kind of tells you."

But Tebow, at least outwardly, seemed unaffected by the mountains of scorn or the hills of praise. Cer-

tainly, not against Pittsburgh.

Tebow fired a pass that Thomas caught in stride. There was the Thomas catch, the Thomas stiff-arm, the Thomas speed and the Thomas touchdown. "Goose" was right. This one play was it.

Of the 10 completions for 316 yards thrown by Tebow, four were to Thomas for 204 yards.

"I know what they're going to say next week," Broncos running back Willis McGahee said of Tebow's critical observers following the Steelers game.

And what is that?

"Can he do it again?" McGahee said.

No, Tebow couldn't do it again.

THE BRONCOS HAD NO ANSWER FOR BRADY, WHO THREW FOR A PLAYOFF RECORD-TYING SIX TOUCHDOWNS. *AAron Ontiveroz, The Denver Post*

end Aaron Hernandez. Apparently, no Bronco can cover Hernandez. When the Broncos played the Pats four weeks ago, Hernandez roamed free most of the afternoon, finishing with nine catches for 129 yards and a touchdown. And his quarterback, Tom Brady, missed the open Hernandez at least two other times, once in the end zone.

More than any team the Broncos' defense has played this year, the Patriots present a matchup problem. For proof, there was the Patriots' 41-23 victory over the Broncos on Dec. 18 in Denver.

• • •

Brady threw for 320 yards, two touchdowns and a 117.3 rating in his first game against the Broncos. In this one, he would pass for 363 yards, as well as tie an NFL postseason record with six touchdown passes – all before the game was four minutes old in the second half. His numbers were so large that despite throwing an interception that led to the Broncos' only touchdown, his rating computed to 137.6.

Gronkowski had three touchdown receptions in the first half. He finished with 10 catches for 145 yards. Hernandez had a 43-yard run from the tailback position and a 17-yard touchdown catch as a tight end.

This would not be Tebow's type of game. He was down 7-0 before he could remove his parka. With Brady operating a no-huddle offense, the Patriots' first drive was absurdly easy, 80 yards in less than two minutes.

Tebow and McGahee, in an attempt to slow down the game and keep the Patriots' offense on the sideline, methodically drove to the New England 37 on their first possession. But as Tebow was about to throw, he was strip-sacked by Patriots linebacker Rob Ninkovich, and the turnover pretty much spoiled any chance the Broncos had of hanging with Brady's fast-moving machine.

Perhaps Tebow's elongated delivery was a factor. Any time Tebow

THE DENVER POST 133

WILL TO WIN: CHAPTER 12

TEBOW COMPLETED JUST 9-OF-26 PASSES WHILE BEING SACKED FIVE TIMES. TRAILING 7-0, TEBOW FUMBLED IN PATRIOTS TERRITORY, TURNING THE BALL OVER TO BRADY, WHO QUICKLY UPPED THE SCORE TO 14-0. *John Leyba, The Denver Post*

gets whacked from behind on his arm, his delivery will come into question. What's known for sure was that Ninkovich blew past rookie right tackle Orlando Franklin.

Brady started 8-of-8 for 79 yards and two touchdowns on his first two drives. Down 14-0, the rest of the game went a tad too fast for Tebow. He dealt with consistent pressure from up the middle and his blind, right side, and he completed just 9-of-26 passes while taking five sacks. Early in the third quarter, Tebow was crushed by a Patriots sandwich of Vince Wilfork and Ninkovich.

The Denver quarterback later found out he had suffered a bruised chest, a bruised right (non-throwing) shoulder and torn rib cartilage.

Tebow nearly came out of the game after that hit, and Broncos coach John Fox had backup Brady Quinn warming up. But Tebow stayed in, saying later: "Sometimes you get hit. Sometimes it can hurt a little bit. But I wanted to play that game."

Sometimes, the characteristics of a winner are best exhibited in defeat.

The Broncos may have earned the right to get in the playoffs. But they more than met their match in New England.

A few Broncos players believed the Patriots benefited from adding St. Louis offensive coordinator and former Denver head coach Josh McDaniels to their staff in the days leading up to the game. The Pats' defense seemed to perfectly time the Broncos' silent count as they gashed through the middle with stunts and blitzes.

However, even had the offense executed well and Tebow played one of his better games, the Patriots still would have won by – what – 60-28? The Broncos simply didn't have the defensive personnel to cover Gronkowski and Hernandez. One series into the third quarter, the Pats pulled back with their 42 points, settling for a 45-10 victory.

The defensive and protection woes didn't stop the divided fan bases – both in Denver and nationally – from questioning how far the Broncos could go with Tebow at quarterback. Tebow proved he could break the Broncos' playoff drought. But now that they tasted the playoffs again, Bronco fans were greedy for more.

Could Tebow go further? His critics were as loud after the playoff loss to the Patriots as Tebow supporters were vocal after the playoff win against the Steelers.

After going 7-1 with 10 touchdown passes and just two interceptions through his first eight starts, Tebow had completed a disconcerting 49-of-120 (40.8 percent) with three touchdown passes and four interceptions in his final five starts. Worse, the Broncos were 1-4 in those final five games, the same record they had under Kyle Orton to begin the season.

Tebow seemed to have the starting quarterback job for 2012 clinched at various times during the season, including as late as after the Steelers playoff game.

But with his rough performances late, and the Broncos about to enter an offseason where they would try to upgrade their roster through free agency and the draft, would Elway, Fox and Xanders go forward with Tebow in 2012?

At high noon Monday, Jan. 16, two days after the fiasco in Foxborough, the Broncos' three-headed management team held a season-ending news conference.

The first question was directed to Elway, and the subject was Tebow's future.

TEBOW TOOK A BRUTAL BEATING FROM THE PATRIOTS DEFENSE. *John Leyba, The Denver Post*

WILL TO WIN: CHAPTER 13

PROGRESS, A PLAYOFF WIN AND GUTTY DETERMINATION EARN TEBOW THE 2012 NOD

Shortly after the media viewing of a Broncos practice begins, coach John Fox walks over to where The Denver Post's Jeff Legwold and Lindsay H. Jones are standing and shoots the bull. Darren "D-Mac" McKee of sports-talk station 104.3 FM, and ESPN's Ed Werder, who has been around the team's Dove Valley headquarters enough since the start of the Tebow phenomenon that he considers the Broncos to be among his "beats," will also mosey into the discussion.

Fox will swap old stories about players he's coached and coaches he's worked for. He'll talk about restaurants, Christmas, places he's lived, wife, kids. The refs. And whatever story the media is blowing up that week.

Almost every day since Fox benched Kyle Orton at halftime of the Broncos' home game against the San Diego Chargers back in early October, Tebow has been a hot-button discussion. Discussion? More like a debate.

Two days after the season ended, four members of the Broncos' front office – Elway, Fox, GM Brian Xanders and media relations director Patrick Smyth – walked down the steps in the team's auditorium. All were wearing sports jackets with opened-collared dress shirts. Elway strode to the table placed on the stage and sat in the center seat. Fox sat to his right, Xanders to his left.

A large contingent of media occupied more than half the seats. Smyth stood to the side and opened it up for questions. The three men in front were still fidgeting for comfort when D-Mac startled the gathering with a booming question from a back row.

ELWAY SAID TEBOW HAD EARNED THE STARTING QUARTERBACK JOB HEADING INTO TRAINING CAMP. *Helen H. Richardson, The Denver Post*

WILL TO WIN: CHAPTER 13

> "I think you have to be the same guy when they said I'd never play an NFL game. Same guy when we had our six-game win streak, same guy when we beat the Steelers, same guy when we got blown out by the Patriots."
>
> Tim Tebow

Said D-Mac: "All the teams in the playoffs, with the possible exception of the Houston Texans, know their quarterback will be their starting quarterback in 2012 and beyond. Are you ready to make a similar commitment to Tim Tebow?"

There it was. No small-talk. No ice-breaking jokes. Bam. Get it out there. The question everyone had been discussing all season, in particular in the two days following the Broncos' 45-10, season-ending loss at New England, was at the front of the news conference and center of the table.

Elway was prepared.

"I think Tim has earned the right to be the starting quarterback going into training camp next year," Elway said. "I think that he made some good strides this year. He obviously played very well against Pittsburgh and played very well in a lot of football games. So ... he has earned the right to be the starter going into training camp next year."

It was the strongest endorsement of Tebow to date by the Broncos' hierarchy.

"Nice," Tebow said the next day in the team's cafeteria. "It's a great honor to be a quarterback for the Denver Broncos. I take that very seriously."

Some didn't think Elway went far enough. Some were glad he didn't take it further. Unequivocal support would have been proclaiming Tebow the Broncos' starting quarterback in the first game of the 2012 season.

Elway, Fox and Xanders were in a tough spot.

Tebow deserved an opening-day guarantee based on the fact he took a team that was 4-12 last season, and 1-4 to start this season, and promptly led it to the playoffs thanks to several incredulous final-minute victories during a 7-1 run. And then, in the playoffs, he played magnificently in an upset win over Pittsburgh.

Quarterbacks have been announced as opening-day starters with far less accomplishments.

But based on Tebow completing just 40.8 percent of his passes in the final five games – in a league where 60 percent is average – he needs to show more improvement before greater promises can be made. Quarterbacks have done more and not received first-game endorsements, too.

"I don't care," Tebow said. "You have to go out there and compete, anyway."

Elway, Fox and Xanders went as far as they could supporting Tebow while stopping short of 100 percent commitment.

Declaring Tebow the starting quarterback through the entire offseason, though, was not insignificant. Free agency opens in mid-March, and even if the Broncos signed a veteran quarterback, Tebow would be No. 1 when team conditioning began a month later on April 16.

The draft would be held in late April, but even if the Broncos selected a quarterback somewhere between the second and fifth rounds, Tebow would be the starter through the organized team activities (OTA) and minicamps that would begin in late May and run through June.

Knowing he's the starting quarterback through the offseason also frees Tebow to take a few more subtle steps toward becoming the team's leader. Tebow takes leadership seriously.

As the youngest of five children, Tebow has been around leaders all his life. His dad led not only his family but has long run ministries. Tebow also has been on enough teams and in enough locker rooms to know what causes people to follow and what causes them to roll their eyes.

Contrary to what people might think from the fiery spirit Tebow exhibits on the field, he is not a vocal, rah-rah type person in the locker room.

"It can't be something that's forced," Tebow said. "It's how you act. Just because you've been given a position of leadership doesn't mean they're going to follow you. You want guys to follow you and want to play with you. I think you have to be yourself and be real.

"I think you have to be the same guy when they said I'd never play an NFL game. Same guy when we had our six-game win streak, same guy when we beat the Steelers, same

ELWAY BELIEVES AN NFL QUARTERBACK HAS TO OPERATE SUCCESSFULLY IN THE POCKET TO WIN. *Tim Rasmussen, The Denver Post*

guy when we got blown out by the Patriots.

"I'm still going to be the first one in and last one to leave. It doesn't matter how many sprints we run, I'm going to run all of them hard. When they realize it's not something I do for show, or not something I do for the media, then they'll know this guy is for real. And then I think they respect you for that. And then you can start to build relationships. Hopefully, that can kind of happen."

There are some knowledgeable NFL observers who don't believe Tebow can ever resolve his passing issues. A throwing motion is a throwing motion. Accuracy is something you have or you don't.

"Why would they say that?" Fox said following the season-ending news conference. "Look how much he improved just this year."

At just about the time the Broncos waived Orton, Elway and Fox had committed to Tebow for the start of the 2012 season. They knew fans and media wanted them to proclaim Tebow as their franchise quarterback. But they did not want to make any such pronouncements during the season. Their plan all along was to endorse Tebow at season's end.

As Elway sat behind his office desk in early December, it was obvious the organization would go forward with Tebow.

"The hardest thing in changing the culture or changing a losing team to becoming respectable or being where we are – you can draft good players, right?" Elway said. "I mean everyone is going to get the same shot at the players, so we can draft better talent. But we needed to change the mind-set of the players to where they were feeling they can win. And when things get tight, you want to change the culture from, 'What bad is going to happen now?' to 'Something good is about to happen.'

"That's the hardest thing to change, and Tebow changed it. No doubt. He was positive. He battled. And he was tough. And any time a team sees their quarterback being a football

| WILL TO WIN: CHAPTER 13

ELWAY WILL HAVE THE EAR OF OWNER PAT BOWLEN AND IS DRIVEN TO ACHIEVE THE ULTIMATE GOAL, ANOTHER SUPER BOWL. HE WILL LOOK TO PUT THE PLAYERS ON THE FIELD WHO GIVE THE BRONCOS THEIR BEST CHANCE TO WIN. FOR NOW, THAT INCLUDES TEBOW. *John Leyba, The Denver Post*

player, they like that."

The Broncos will add a quarterback this offseason, maybe two. And they won't necessarily be quarterbacks who can back up Tebow and run the read option. Tebow's backup likely will be a more conventional quarterback, one with more polished passing skills.

The read-option offense helped Tebow acclimate to the NFL. Eventually, Tebow will have to become better from the pocket to keep his position.

Elway said he's going to call on his own experiences as the Broncos' quarterback from 1983-98 as a teaching tool for Tebow.

"I want to help Tim to improve through what I learned," Elway said. "I was a mobile guy when I was young but probably at times moved too much and relied too much on moving around. I finally realized a little bit later in my career that I wished I'd learned – the fact that you do have to win from the pocket. Most of our success came when I was in the pocket."

Tim Tebow's 2011 season taught the football universe that a quarterback can succeed even if he can't always pass well. He also demonstrated that there is backlash to enormous fame.

"I wouldn't like it except it gives me a chance to help kids," Tebow said once at his locker during the season. "I'll say this: Just as many things that might be negative about it, there have been 20 more that have been positive."

Above all, Tebow reminded fans that the human spirit cannot be underestimated. It's not necessarily corny or hokey to say a team or individual won because they wanted it more. Tebow showed it could happen. And, for a while there, all he did was win.

"You look into the future, and what people don't understand is, if he is the guy, his type of guy isn't easy to find," Elway said. "Especially with the intangibles he has. We can't teach intangibles. You either have them or you don't. He has them.

"Now, can you fix some of the passing issues? You can fix the feet. The release is the release. You can tweak a few things, but that's naturally how he throws. You're not going to change the nature of his release. But you can change the feet. And to get him to understand how his clock and his progressions are tied to his feet."

Elway said he is going to work with Tebow during the offseason. He is going to work on his footwork, starting with his drop.

"You can't be accurate backing up trying to throw," Elway said. "You're accurate when you're throwing on rhythm moving forward.

"He's got plenty of arm. When it's longer like that, you have to anticipate a little bit more. He doesn't always have confidence in that yet. He will. The only way to get it is to keep playing. There's no substitute for experience."

Ask an athlete about their future and most of them can't really envision past the next season. They all believe they're going to have 15-year careers. And then when they get to Year 15, they believe they'll be the exception and make it to 20.

There is so much more in Tebow's future. Although there was a decent chance he could have played in the Pro Bowl as a second alternate, his bruised ribs, chest and non-throwing shoulder were not going to allow him to participate.

As soon as his battered body rests up, he plans to resume his workouts with performance coach Loren Landow, whom he met through conditioning drills organized by teammate Brian Dawkins last summer.

"I'm not a guy that at all will be

TEBOW CERTAINLY BRINGS THE EXCITEMENT – AND THE TEBOW MANIACS. *John Leyba, The Denver Post*

trusting, especially when you're dealing with my body," Tebow said of Landow. "And when the team started working out with him, I was as hesitant as anybody because I'm not going to let someone hurt me or affect my body in a bad way. But just through time, he definitely earned my trust with him as a trainer and as a friend, too. He's good at what he does."

For Tebow, there is so much more to his future than offseason workouts or the 2012 season. Football has given him an enormous platform to affect others. He often says he doesn't know what the future holds, but he knows who holds his future.

"One of my favorites," he said.

Has God delivered any hints as to what his future might hold after football?

"Good question," Tebow said. "I think my passion is growing for my foundation. I always wanted to be involved in helping people. But to see where our foundation has gone, I know for the rest of my life I'm going to be involved with that. I don't know if someday I want to get into politics. I don't know if someday I want to get into business."

Another thought. How about following in dad's footsteps and creating Tim Tebow Ministries? Only in Tim's case, his ministries can go global. It's not difficult to envision Tim Tebow in a pulpit delivering sermons to enormous congregations and televised to millions at home.

Is it so far-fetched to see Tebow one day becoming the next Billy Graham?

"One of the coolest things I've had is Billy Graham did reach out to me during the season," Tebow said. "He wants me to fly and go see him. I'm going to try to make that happen."

Graham, 93, is the most famous Christian evangelist in American history.

"You talk about someone, obviously people now give him praise and he's well regarded, but you talk about someone who got bashed a lot?" Tebow said. "He overcame a lot of adversity. Not a lot of people liked what he was saying because he was very much a straight shooter with it."

Sounds familiar.